CENTENNIAL EDITION

This edition published in 2017
By Thomas Allen & Son Ltd
195 Allstate Parkway
Markham, ON L3R 4T8

First published in 2008; Second Edition 2011; Third Edition 2014

ISBN: 978-1-77328-148-3

Editor: Martin Corteel
Assistant Editor: David Ballheimer
Design & Art Direction: Stephen Cary
Design, Layout & Imaging: Jörn Kröger
Photography: Craig Campbell;
    Karl Adamson; Matthew Manor,
    Manor Photographic Imaging
Picture Research: Paul Langan
Production: Lisa French

Printed in China

**Dan Diamond with Eric Zweig and
Craig Ellenport**

with a foreword by Gary B. Bettman NHL Commissioner

CENTENNIAL EDITION

The Official
NHL Hockey Treasures

THOMAS
ALLEN & SON
SINCE 1916

Contents

Foreword

Our year-long 2017 Centennial Celebration commemorates a century of great players, outstanding teams and landmark arenas. The NHL's grand history spans unforgettable moments, countless thrills, exceptional performances and the matchless drama of the quest for the Stanley Cup – the most cherished trophy in sports.

From the richness of the "Original Six" era to the stories of some of our game's most famous families – including the Howes, Hulls, Richards, Espositos and Sutters – **The Official NHL Hockey Treasures** traces all the elements of our League's development and evolution. In addition to the stories and images, this volume includes a bonus: reproductions of documents and artifacts that represent special moments in League history.

The Official NHL Hockey Treasures takes you back to the inception of our League in 1917. It provides insight into the thoughts and theories of

hockey's most successful coaches. It offers a perfect vantage point for our groundbreaking Winter Classic, Heritage Classic and Stadium Series outdoor games. It outlines the influences that have helped make the NHL the best pro hockey League in the world.

As we honor our history, celebrate our present and look forward to a bright future, **The Official NHL Hockey Treasures** is your personal reference resource for every fascinating detail. I am delighted, on behalf of the National Hockey League, to welcome you to this unique reading experience.

Enjoy!

Gary B. Bettman
Commissioner

The 2017 NHL All-Star Game was also a celebration of the NHL's 100 greatest players.

Introduction

Welcome to **The Official NHL Hockey Treasures**, a book that celebrates and illustrates the premiere league in the world's fastest game. It is all here, from the roots of the game, when hockey first moved indoors from frozen lakes and rivers to the huge "event" games of today where hockey has moved outdoors again into giant parks and stadiums. Along the way there's the NHL's opening faceoff in Montreal on December 19, 1917, through the sport's various dynasties and golden eras to the young superstars of today's high-speed international game and their competition to make their dreams come true by winning the glittering Stanley Cup.

The Official NHL Hockey Treasures is rich and multi-layered, using words, photographs of on-ice action and objects from all eras of hockey to tell the story of the NHL. These objects – ticket stubs, trophies, trading cards, equipment, program covers, pucks and player contracts – evoke the courage of men who played the game in every era of the NHL.

And in addition to photographs of unique objects, this book includes beautifully reproduced facsimiles of cherished hockey items. Some are of great significance. These include a hastily written note by NHL president Clarence Campbell dated March 17, 1955. In it he informs Detroit general manager Jack Adams that a smoke bomb and unruly fans both inside and outside the Montreal Forum have forced cancellation and a forfeit of the game. Adams is advised to take his players from the arena and you can sense the menace in the air at that moment.

There's a contract with the Montreal Canadiens signed by "Bad" Joe Hall for the 1918–19 season. Hall was a veteran defenseman and a professional player from the very earliest days of play-for-pay hockey. That season, he was part of the Canadiens team that played in the only incomplete Stanley Cup Final, as the series was suspended after five games because Spanish Influenza was rampant and many players were ill. Tragically, Hall was hospitalized and never recovered, passing away on April 5, 1919.

Also included is a remarkable unsigned pencil drawing of a proposed redesign for the Stanley Cup trophy. Canada's Governor-General donated the silver bowl that sits atop today's glittering column in 1893, but the trophy grew in fits and starts, a ring here and a new band there, in the intervening 121 years. This proposal was probably drawn in the mid to late 1950s, and is a slightly scaled down version of the big five-band barrel that made its debut in 1958 and gives the trophy its distinctive silhouette and balance. Perfect for hoisting overhead in triumph!

Add to these items a comic book from 1947 and a telegram from 1901 and hockey cards, schedule pamphlets and ticket stubs from every era, and the collection lives up to its name as Treasures of the National Hockey League.

Wishing you much enjoyment from this wonderful book,

Dan Diamond, Eric Zweig, and Craig Ellenport
Toronto, April 2017

Many of the men included in the 100 Greatest NHL Players appeared at the NHL Centennial Gala.

Chapter 1
Origins of the NHL

The sport of hockey as we know it today evolved over hundreds of years from lawn games played in Europe. It wasn't until the late 1800s that the game moved onto ice. Amateur leagues took shape, featuring teams such as the Montreal AAA and Ottawa's Silver Seven. The American Hockey Association and Pacific Coast Hockey Association emerged as two main forces in the sport, and an aristocrat named Lord Stanley gave them a trophy to play for.

An early game at McGill University: pond hockey comes to the city.

The Origins Debate

Where did hockey begin? The true origins of the game are difficult to determine. Modern hockey first moved indoors off frozen lakes and rivers in the city of Montreal in 1875. Although the rules and equipment were very different, today's fans would still recognize the game of the late 19th century.

1

The origins of hockey have been the subject of much debate for many years. Early contenders include the frozen lakes and rivers around Windsor and Halifax, Nova Scotia, and the harbor in Kingston, Ontario. It is apparent that rudimentary forms of hockey based on British ball-and-stick games were played in Nova Scotia around the turn of the 19th century. Then again, there is plenty of evidence, particularly in Dutch paintings, of people playing hockey-like games on ice in Europe in the 16th century.

In any discussion of the origins of hockey, one thing becomes clear. The game was not truly "invented" anywhere. It evolved over a lengthy period of time. In 1943, Professor Emanuel M. Orlick, an assistant director of physical education at McGill University in Montreal, wrote a series of articles on the origins of hockey for the *Montreal Gazette* and the *McGill News*. Orlick raised the key issue when he wrote: "The question is not when the games of field hockey, hoquet, hurley or shinny started, but rather, when and where did hurley or shinny develop into the game of Ice Hockey as we know it today?"

The best evidence as to the early development of "modern" hockey points to Montreal, where the sport first came indoors off frozen lakes

and rivers for a demonstration at Montreal's Victoria Skating Rink on March 3, 1875.

James George Aylwin Creighton, a native of Halifax who moved to Montreal in 1872 and graduated from McGill law school in 1880, is said to have drafted some informal rules for "ice hockey" in 1873 after he and some other friends tried to play lacrosse on skates in the Victoria rink. Creighton later captained one of the teams that played in the world's first public display of indoor ice hockey. Though it is likely that Creighton and the others who took part in it had been playing hockey for some time,

2

1: Hockey had spread all across Canada by the 1890s. The January 1896 edition of *The Canadian Magazine* featured a story on hockey in the North-West.

2: Paintings such as this one depict people enjoying games played on ice in The Netherlands in the 16th century.

3: A vast sheet of outdoor ice, goal posts with no nets and tiny dasher boards around the rink were hallmarks of 1880s hockey at McGill University in Montreal.

3

The Victoria Rink

Montreal's Victoria Skating Club was incorporated on June 9, 1862, soon to be followed by the Victoria Skating Rink, which opened its doors on Christmas Eve, December 24, 1862. It wasn't the first indoor rink in Montreal, but it quickly became the most important.

Named in honor of Queen Victoria, the rink faced Drummond Street and backed onto Stanley, just north of Dorchester (now Rene Levesque Boulevard) in the center of elite, English Montreal. Today, the site is not far from the Bell Center, where the Montreal Canadiens play.

The Victoria Skating Club, and the Rink, drew its patrons predominantly from the city's upper class. The costume balls and skating carnivals held at the Rink were important events on the Montreal social calendar for decades. With its decorative curved trusses supporting a high-pitched roof, the rink was elegant indeed, though the low boards measuring just a few inches high were not particularly well suited to hockey, which became a regular feature during the 1880s and '90s.

the first indoor exhibition (played on a surface that measured 200 feet by 85, setting a standard that remains in place today) required several key modifications. Most importantly, the ball that was traditionally used was cut flat to prevent it from flying into the crowd. Goal posts (though no net) were employed, and a player was positioned in front of the net to try and keep the flattened ball (the term "puck" came later) from passing between the posts. The teams that evening had nine men on the ice and, borrowing

from the rules of rugby, were not allowed to make forward passes. The puck could be advanced only by skating and stickhandling.

Within ten years of the first indoor game, hockey had begun to transform itself from novelty act to major sport. The game was featured at the first Montreal Winter Carnival in 1883, and it was there that teams began using seven players on the ice. (The seventh player was known as the "rover.") In 1885 Canada's first league was organized in Kingston. It involved four local teams. The first inter-regional league was formed in the winter of 1886–87 as an offshoot of the annual Montreal Winter Carnival competitions. Four Montreal teams—the Victorias, McGill, the Crystals, and the Montreal Amateur Athletic Association—plus a team from Ottawa (which would not reappear in the league again until 1891) formed the Amateur Hockey Association of Canada. The Quebec City Hockey Club joined the league in 1888–89.

Soon other leagues began to spring up in provinces across Canada, including the Ontario Hockey Association, which was organized on November 27, 1890, and signaled Toronto's formal entry into the hockey scene. But the AHAC remained the country's dominant hockey loop until 1898–99, when the Canadian Amateur Hockey League replaced it. This began the evolution of the AHAC into the NHL.

If a hockey fan took a time machine and traveled back to the 1890s, that fan might have a hard time recognizing the game. Goalies were only just starting to wear pads on their legs, while the other players used very little visible protection. They may have had catalogues or magazines under their socks and tucked a little something extra into their football-style pants. They wore long woolen socks and thick sweaters for warmth in drafty wooden arenas that relied on cold temperatures to keep the ice frozen. Many players also wore woolen hats. There were no hockey helmets or special hockey gloves, and games began when the referee placed the puck on the ice between two opposing centers and shouted, "Play!" The seven men who started the game were expected to finish it, with substitutions allowed only in cases of severe injury. Goalies had to remain standing at all times.

4: Even after hockey formally moved indoors, backyard rinks and other outdoor facilities remained the game's training grounds (and playgrounds) for decades.

5: Boys choose up sides for a game played on a frozen river.

Interest in the game spread after the creation of the Cup. At first , it was an amateur challenge trophy which the champion defended when called upon. By 1914, the Stanley Cup Final was an annual battle between the champions of the game's top professional leagues.

1

The history of the Stanley Cup prior to the formation of the NHL in 1917 tells the story of how hockey grew from a regionalized amateur pastime into a professional business.

As a gift to the country and the sport he came to love during his term as Canada's Governor General, Lord Stanley of Preston announced in 1892 that he would donate a national championship trophy. His Stanley Cup was first presented to the Montreal Hockey Club (more commonly known as the Montreal AAA because of its affiliation with the Montreal Amateur Athletic Association) as champions of the Amateur Hockey Association of Canada in 1893.

Since Lord Stanley wanted his cup to represent a national championship, he instructed trustees Philip Dansken Ross and John Sweetland to establish terms allowing teams in leagues all across the country to challenge for the trophy. In February of 1896, the Winnipeg Victorias of the Manitoba and NorthWest Hockey Association became the first successful challengers. Winnipeg goaltender George "Whitey" Merritt caused a huge sensation when he showed up wearing white cricket pads. It was the first time a goalie had worn leg padding during a Stanley Cup match, and Merritt blanked the Montreal Victorias 2–0. Interest in hockey reached a new peak when the Montreal Victorias headed west to Winnipeg in December and won back the Stanley Cup in a rematch.

The Ottawa Hockey Club, commonly known as the Ottawas at the time but best known today as the Silver Seven, were Stanley Cup champions for three straight seasons when they helped to form the

Eastern Canada Amateur Hockey Association in 1905–06. Ottawa's run as Stanley Cup champions ended when the team lost their league title to the Montreal Wanderers in March 1906. In November of that year, the Wanderers and Ottawa played a key role in ushering in a new era in Stanley Cup history. At the ECAHA annual meeting prior to the 1906–07 season, the teams pushed through a resolution allowing professional players to play alongside amateurs.

4

1: Brothers Lester (left) and Frank Patrick (right) starred with the NHA's Renfrew Millionaires before forming the PCHA.

2: Gold pocket watch presented to Joe Hall by the city of Quebec after the Quebec Bulldogs won the Stanley Cup in 1912.

3: The Stanley Cup as it originally appeared from 1893 to 1908. It began to grow larger with the addition of a second ring below the bowl in 1909.

4: The 1905 Ottawa Hockey Club. Known today as the Silver Seven, the Ottawas were the first great dynasty of the 20th century.

5: The 1896 Winnipeg Victorias. Note Whitey Merritt's cricket pads.

2

3

5

6

The issue of professionalism was a hot topic in Canada and around the sporting world at this time. Many people clung to the British aristocratic tradition of sports for sports' sake, but the truth was that many hockey players had been paid to play for many years—though these payments were usually made in secret. The first openly professional hockey league was the International Hockey League, which operated with teams in Pennsylvania, Michigan, and northwestern Ontario, from 1904 to 1907.

6: The 1893 Montreal AAA Hockey Club was the first Stanley Cup champion.

7: Billy Barlow's Stanley Cup ring from 1893.

8: Commemorative trophy presented to Art Ross by the citizens of Kenora after the Kenora Thistles won the Stanley Cup in 1907.

9: Team picture of the Seattle Metropolitans, the first Stanley Cup champions from the United States.

7

8

9

Lord Stanley

Frederick Arthur, Lord Stanley of Preston, the 16th Earl of Derby, was born in London on January 15, 1841. The son of a three-time Prime Minister of England, he served in Parliament from 1865 to 1886. He also sat in the House of Lords and spent a short stint as the Secretary of State for the British Colonies. He was appointed Governor General of Canada in 1888.

Like most British aristocrats, Lord Stanley was an avid sportsman. He and his family enjoyed the new sports they discovered during his posting to Ottawa. Sons Arthur and Algernon and daughter Isobel were particularly fond of hockey. An aide of Lord Stanley's purchased the original Stanley Cup bowl from a London silversmith for ten guineas (about $51.10), but Lord Stanley was called back to England in the midst of the 1893 hockey season and never saw his Cup presented. He passed away at Holwood on June 14, 1908.

Though the issue remained contentious, the Stanley Cup trustees (now P. D. Ross and William Foran) agreed to let the Stanley Cup become the emblem of professional hockey supremacy.

In 1909–10, a new professional league emerged as Canada's top hockey circuit. The National Hockey Association (forerunner of the NHL) introduced the Montreal Canadiens to the game during its inaugural season. In 1910–11 the NHA changed the timing of hockey games from two 30-minute halves to three 20-minute periods. Prior to the 1911–12 season, the NHA eliminated the position of rover and introduced the six-man game.

Another important change was introduced to hockey in 1911–12 when brothers Frank and Lester Patrick formed the Pacific Coast Hockey Association. In addition to running the league, Frank served as a player, coach, general manager, and owner of the PCHA's Vancouver Millionaires. Lester held the same duties with the Victoria Aristocrats. (It was hoped the monied monikers would lend the league a touch of class.) The Patricks were innovators, and while it was the NHA that would one day become the NHL it was the PCHA that truly modernized hockey. The PCHA introduced artificial ice rinks to Canada, and though Frank and Lester stubbornly maintained the position of rover, they painted blue lines on the ice, legalized forward passing, and permitted goaltenders to leave their feet. In all, some 20 rules proposed by Frank Patrick eventually found their way into NHL rulebooks.

Though the two leagues fought at first, the NHA and the PCHA signed a "peace treaty" in the fall of 1913 that included an agreement for the two league champions to meet in an annual playoff beginning in 1914. Despite stories that the Stanley Cup trustees were against it, they agreed to let the Stanley Cup be used as the prize in the so-called "World Series" of Hockey.

Another significant development in Stanley Cup history took place when the PCHA's New Westminster Royals franchise left British Columbia for Oregon, where it became the Portland Rosebuds in 1914–15. (Portland is known as "The Rose City.") There was now the possibility of an American-based team playing for the Stanley Cup, which had always been emblematic of Canadian supremacy. In December of 1915, the trustees formally announced that they were agreeable to this situation. The Rosebuds won the PCHA title in 1916, but lost the Stanley Cup Final to the Montreal Canadiens. One year later, the Seattle Metropolitans beat the Canadiens and the Stanley Cup headed south of the border for the very first time.

Birth of a League

1

Canadian involvement in World War I had professional hockey in a state of flux. Bickering among hockey owners made things worse. As the War in Europe raged on, a group of owners reorganized the NHA in November of 1917 and called their new creation the National Hockey League.

Professional hockey was in a sorry state when the National Hockey League was founded from the ashes of National Hockey Association in November of 1917. Several crises had erupted during the NHA season of 1916–17 and the six-team circuit barely survived. All disagreements were particularly bitter due to the unique circumstances of operating during a world war. With more and more men enlisting for the armed forces, or scrambling for exempt positions in munitions plants and other vital industries, player shortages already had some franchises facing withdrawal from the league.

Further complicating every problem in the NHA was the lingering battle between the owners of the Montreal Canadiens, the Montreal Wanderers, the Ottawa Senators and the Quebec Bulldogs on one side, and Edward J. Livingstone, owner of the Toronto Blueshirts, on the other.

Eddie Livingstone was an outsider to professional hockey, having learned the game in the amateur Ontario Hockey Association. He used his old contacts to help stock his teams with previously unknown amateur players and this did not sit well with his fellow owners. Nor did the fact that Livingstone seemed to enjoy butting heads with them, accusing them of everything from poor sportsmanship to poor business practices. So it was not surprising that when the 228th Battalion team, which had entered the NHA for the 1916–17 season, was summoned for overseas service midway through the schedule, that Livingstone and his fellow owners could not come to an agreement on a solution.

One day after the 228th Battalion withdrew from the NHA on February 10, 1917, NHA owners met in Montreal to determine how to salvage the season. Livingstone was unable to attend due to illness, yet he

sent his instructions to NHA president Frank Robinson. These instructions were completely ignored when the other teams chose to eliminate Toronto from the league. After three years of bucking the traditional powers in Ottawa and Montreal, Livingstone was dumped without compensation and his players were redistributed among the remaining clubs.

Livingstone screamed loud and long about the treatment he'd received, launching lawsuits that dragged into the 1930s. His actions only seemed to make the other owners even more determined to rid themselves of this troublesome Torontonian. The die was cast when Frank Robinson resigned as NHA president on September 29, 1917. Livingstone no longer had any allies at the league level and, as a series of meetings was held throughout November, it became fairly clear that he was being frozen out. To achieve this end, the Senators, Canadiens, Wanderers and Bulldogs suspended the NHA and started a new league.

Over the years, November 22, 1917, has usually been given as the formation date for the National Hockey League. However, the meetings originally scheduled for that day were postponed, first until

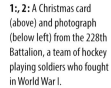

3

1:, 2: A Christmas card (above) and photograph (below left) from the 228th Battalion, a team of hockey playing soldiers who fought in World War I.

3: A pocket watch presented to Goldie Prodger by the citizens of Victoria after

the PCHA's Victoria Cougars won the unofficial world's professional championship in 1913.

4: Frank Calder at his desk. The former secretary of the National Hockey Association was the founding president of the NHL.

2

4

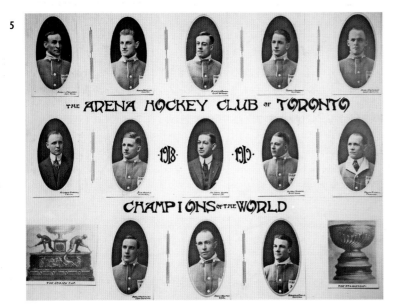

THE ARENA HOCKEY CLUB OF TORONTO

·1918· ·1919·

CHAMPIONS OF THE WORLD

5: Team picture of the 1919 Toronto Arenas club that won the Stanley Cup during the NHL's first season of 1917–18.

6: A gold locket presented to Goldie Prodger after winning the Stanley Cup with the Quebec Bulldogs in 1912.

Joe Malone

A member of the Quebec Bulldogs for most of his career, Joe Malone became property of the Montreal Canadiens when the NHL began. He went on to lead the league with an astounding 44 goals in just 20 games during the inaugural season of 1917–18.

Malone was already a scoring star before the birth of the NHL. In 1912–13, he led the NHA with 43 goals, and added nine more in a single Stanley Cup game when the Bulldogs won their second straight championship. Malone tied for a second NHA scoring title with 41 goals in 1916–17. He won a second NHL scoring title after returning to the Bulldogs in 1919–20. Among his 39 goals that year were seven in a single game on January 31, 1920 for an NHL record that still stands.

Nicknamed "Phantom," Joe Malone was a slick stickhandler and a deceptive skater. He was elected to the Hockey Hall of Fame in 1950.

November 24, and then to November 26. Had the Quebec Bulldogs not announced that day that they would not ice a team for the 1917–18 season, Toronto might have been frozen out of the NHL too. Faced with the prospect of having franchises in only Ottawa and Montreal, newly elected NHL president Frank Calder (the former the secretary-treasurer of the NHA) stated that a "new" Toronto franchise, owned by "a syndicate of Toronto sportsmen" would be a part of the new league. Because these new hockey owners also operated the city's Arena Gardens rink on Mutual Street, Toronto's inaugural NHL franchise has become known as the Toronto Arenas—though the name did not become official until the 1918–19 season.

Ridding itself of Eddie Livingstone did not mean the NHL was free from problems. World War I was still raging in Europe, and fan interest in hockey was at an all-time low. When the NHL season opened on December 19, 1917, only 700 fans turned out to see the Wanderers' 10–9 victory over Toronto, even though soldiers in uniform were admitted free of charge. Then, the league almost came to pieces on January 2, 1918, when a fire destroyed the Montreal Arena. Wanderers owner Sam Lichtenhein (who had been threatening to withdraw from the league due to a lack of good players) used the arena fire as an excuse to get out of hockey for good, even though the city of Hamilton offered to give his team a home for the rest of the season. The Canadiens, who shared the Arena with the Wanderers, moved into the much smaller Jubilee rink and the NHL struggled along with just three teams: the Canadiens, the Senators and the "Arenas."

Virtually all the players stripped from Livingstone in 1916–17 were back in Toronto for the 1917–18 season and the Blueshirts/Arenas defeated the Canadiens for the first NHL title. They then beat the Vancouver Millionaires of the Pacific Coast Hockey Association to win the 1918 Stanley Cup.

Chapter 2
NHL's Early Years

After World War I ended, interest in hockey exploded, not only throughout Canada but also in the United States. The NHL and other leagues expanded and outstanding players began to gain fame. Rule changes increased scoring and made the game more popular but the Great Depression and World War II led to a contraction of teams and players. Nonetheless, the sport's popularity—fueled by the "Original Six" and players such as Maurice Richard—continued to grow.

Detroit goalie Harry Lumley was 17 when he made his debut in 1943.

The NHL was in transition in the early years. Some teams failed or relocated as the sport stabilized. A new league joined the PCHA in western Canada and the NHL expanded into the United States. After Victoria's 1925 Stanley Cup win, western Canada had a 59-year wait for another one.

As life settled down after World War I, interest in professional hockey increased. In 1919, the Quebec Bulldogs returned to the NHL, reclaiming the players who had been distributed around the league. Yet even with superstar Joe Malone, Quebec won just four games and suffered 20 losses during the 1919–20 season. (The following year, the Bulldogs moved to southern Ontario and become the Hamilton Tigers.)

After a worldwide Influenza Epidemic forced the cancellation of the 1919 Stanley Cup Final, the PCHA champion Seattle Metropolitans trekked to Ottawa to play the Senators for the Stanley Cup in the spring of 1920. When the natural ice in Ottawa's Laurier Avenue arena deteriorated part way through the series, play was shifted to the artificial ice of Toronto's Mutual Street Arena, home of the NHL's Toronto franchise which, in 1919–20, had been renamed the St. Patricks. There, the Senators captured the Stanley Cup. A year later, Ottawa again emerged as the NHL's top club, and the powerhouse Senators journeyed to Vancouver to face the Millionaires before a record 11,000 fans in the opening game of a Stanley Cup series that Ottawa would again win.

As the popularity of professional hockey grew, so did the value of an NHL team. The sale of the Montreal Canadiens, whose roster included established stars such as Newsy Lalonde, Georges Vezina, and brothers Sprague and Odie Cleghorn, became a benchmark for franchise transfers when Leo Dandurand, Joseph Cattarinich, and Louis Letourneau paid $11,000 for the team in November, 1921. Out west, a third major professional hockey league rose to challenge the NHL and the PCHA. The Western Canada Hockey League began play in 1921–22 with the Calgary Tigers, the Edmonton Eskimos, the Regina Capitals and the Saskatoon Sheiks staffed mainly by local players and a smattering of former NHA,

1: Sunday magazine supplement from the *Seattle Times*, January 30, 1921.

2: The 1924–25 Edmonton Eskimos, photographed here in their home rink, finished fourth in the Western Canada Hockey League.

3: The 1920 Ottawa Senators won the first of four Stanley Cup titles the team captured during that decade.

Four NHL stars of the 1920s:
4: Howie Morenz, Montreal
5: Frank Fredrickson, Detroit
6: Dit Clapper , Boston
7: Eddie Shore, Boston.

9

8: Hockey sweater worn by Howie Morenz.

9: Newsy Lalonde, who starred with the Montreal Canadiens before going west to Saskatoon.

10: Seattle Metropolitans jersey worn by future Hall of Famer Frank Foyston in 1923–24.

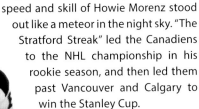

10

teams that season, adding a second franchise in Montreal (the Maroons) and expanding into the United States for the first time.

The NHL had named Thomas Duggan as its U.S. agent back in 1922, and Duggan eventually arranged for a franchise in Boston and, later, in New York. The Boston franchise, owned by local grocery store magnate Charles Adams and run by Art Ross (a former star player who would eventually be one of hockey's best-known administrators) was named the Bruins.

To accommodate the NHL's expansion teams, the regular-season schedule was expanded from 24 to 30 games in 1924–25. But the longer schedule brought on the NHL's first labor dispute. Although Hamilton finished in first place, Tigers players contended that they had signed on to play the old 24-game regular-season schedule and refused to compete in playoff games unless they were given a raise as compensation for the extra six games in the regular season. NHL president Frank Calder responded by suspending all the Hamilton players and ordering the second-place Canadiens and third-place Toronto to play off for the league championship. Soon after, when Duggan found a buyer for his second U.S. franchise, the Tigers players were sold to stock the New York Americans and Hamilton was out of the NHL.

ex-NHL and ex-PCHA players. The most notable of these was Regina's Dick Irvin, a star player who would later gain even more fame as coach of the Montreal Canadiens.

The new WCHL prolonged the careers of older players and opened up new opportunities for younger ones. It also gave NHL owners a new marketplace. Dandurand, tired of quarreling with Newsy Lalonde, attempted to sell his aging superstar to Saskatoon during the 1922–23 season. But NHL president Frank Calder nixed the deal on the grounds that Lalonde hadn't been offered on waivers to other NHL teams. Calder ruled that instead of cash, Dandurand would get the rights to a young Northern Ontario Hockey League player who was on the Saskatoon negotiating list. Dandurand was upset at having to accept Aurel Joliat, though Joliat soon became a major star playing alongside Howie Morenz, who joined the Canadiens from Stratford, Ontario, for the 1923–24 season.

NHL hockey in the 1920s was no game for the faint of heart or body. Padding was so poor that injuries were near constant. Stick swinging was the order of the day and butt-ending was a high art. Contrasted against this, the speed and skill of Howie Morenz stood out like a meteor in the night sky. "The Stratford Streak" led the Canadiens to the NHL championship in his rookie season, and then led them past Vancouver and Calgary to win the Stanley Cup.

In 1922–23, the PCHA and WCHL began playing an interlocking schedule, made possible when the PCHA abandoned the rover position and went from six skaters to five and a goalie like the other two major professional leagues. By the 1924–25 season, the two western leagues had merged into one six-team circuit. The NHL also grew to six

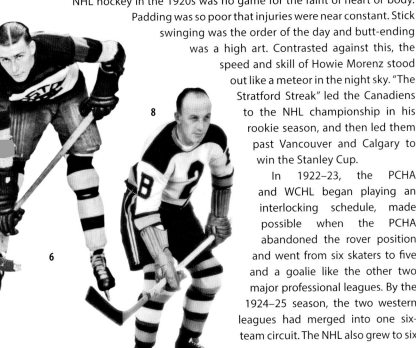

8

6

The Victoria Cougars

Lester Patrick's Victoria franchise hosted the first game in PCHA history in January of 1912. In March 1914, the Aristocrats became the first PCHA team to play for the Stanley Cup. But, like so many in the hockey fraternity, the years of World War I were difficult ones for the Victoria club. Forced to relocate to Spokane, Washington in 1916–17, then to drop out of the league entirely the following year, Victoria was back in 1918–19, but things did not begin to improve until future Hall of Famer and 1920 Olympic gold medalist Frank Fredrickson joined the team for the 1920–21 season.

In 1923–24, the Aristocrats became the Cougars. A year later, Victoria and Vancouver joined the WCHL. Bolstered by Jack Walker and Frank Foyston, two more future Hall of Famers, the Cougars won the WCHL championship in 1924–25 and the Stanley Cup as well. They are the last non-NHL team ever to do so.

WESTERN CHAMPIONS 1924-25   WORLD CHAMPIONS 1924-25

VICTORIA COUGARS

W.C.H.L. CUP   STANLEY CUP

Roaring Twenties

With the collapse of the rival leagues out west, the NHL grew to ten teams in 1926–27. Players from the Western Hockey League were sold to expansion teams in the United States—in big-market cities such as Boston, Chicago, and Detroit, as well as pair in New York City—and the NHL grew in popularity and financial success.

1

The 1920s have been called "The Golden Age of Sports." The Great War was over and a new generation of North Americans was in the mood to celebrate. Music was jazzier, movies began to talk, and the popularity of sports exploded. Babe Ruth hit home runs farther and more often than anyone had ever seen. Red Grange tore up the gridiron at the University of Illinois, and then gave the fledgling National Football League an air of respectability by signing with the Chicago Bears. Boxing had Jack Dempsey and Gene Tunney. Golf had Bobby Jones. Tennis had Bill Tilden and Helen Wills Moody. The NHL was on the upswing too.

The Pittsburgh Pirates and New York Americans followed Boston into the NHL for the 1925–26 season. Hockey was a big hit in the Big Apple, as the Americans drew more fans in their first season than any four teams of the Western Hockey League combined! In Montreal, the Maroons became Stanley Cup champions in just their second

2

season while playing to sellout crowds in the 10,000-seat Montreal Forum. (The Canadiens did not become full-time Forum tenants until 1926–27.)

The NHL was now a financial success and potential owners were lining up to obtain teams in Chicago and Detroit for 1926–27. Tex Rickard also wanted his own New York franchise for Madison Square Garden. The sudden prosperity of the NHL was not lost on the owners of the Western Hockey League. They closed up shop and sold off players to stock the rosters of the new NHL teams in Chicago and Detroit and bulk up other teams like the Rangers and Bruins.

The newly expanded 10-team NHL split into two divisions. The Boston Bruins, Pittsburgh Pirates, New York Rangers, Chicago Blackhawks and Detroit Cougars (later Falcons, then Red Wings) played in the American Division, while the Montreal Canadiens, Montreal Maroons, Ottawa Senators, Toronto St. Pats/Maple Leafs

1: Billy Burch.

2: Aurel Joliat wore this trademark black cap with the Montreal Canadiens between 1922 and 1938.

3: Coach Red Dutton with (left to right) Wilf Field, Harry Watson and Pat Egan of the 1941–42 Brooklyn Americans.

4: Mush March debuted with Chicago in 1928 and would enjoy a 17-year career with the Black Hawks.

5: Bun Cook of the New York Rangers played on a forward line with his brother Bill and Frank Boucher.

3

4

Long before the Rangers–Islanders rivalry that has fueled New York hockey since the 1970s, there was another Big Apple battle for supremacy on the ice. The Rangers, like today, were part of the original rivalry. Back in the 1920s, the other half was the New York Americans.

The Americans began play in the NHL in 1925–26, owned by a notorious New York City bootlegger named "Big Bill" Dwyer, and they played in a brand new arena: Madison Square Garden. When Tex Rickard, owner of Madison Square Garden, saw how popular the Americans were in their inaugural NHL season, he wanted to get in on the action. A year later, he was awarded his own team, the Rangers.

Not only were they rivals in the city, they were rivals under one roof. The difference was that the Rangers were part of the MSG family, whereas the Americans were paying tenants. That fact only added to the intensity of the feud.

With the exception of a thrilling 1938 first-round playoff series victory—capped by a quadruple-overtime win in the deciding game—the Americans were mostly on the short end of the New York–New York rivalry. And, by 1942, the Americans had ceased to exist.

5 and New York Americans played in the Canadian (or International) Division. Both Detroit and Chicago were expected to have new arenas ready as part of their inclusion in the NHL, but experienced delays. The Red Wings spent their first season across the border in Windsor, Ontario, before moving into the Detroit Olympia in 1927–28. The Chicago Stadium was finally ready in December 1929.

With the best available players now in one league, competition in the NHL was better than ever … but scoring was at an all-time low. In 1928–29, George Hainsworth registered 22 shutouts in 44 games while posting a 0.92 goals-against average. In an effort to increase offense, the NHL finally authorized forward passing in all three zones for the 1929–30 season. With a bit of tinkering, the modern offside rules were born. Over the next 10 seasons the NHL incorporated several other rules and innovations (many first introduced by the Patricks in the PCHA) that are still part of the game today.

With the opening of Maple Leaf Gardens and his team's rebuilding project in full swing, Smythe had desperately wanted to acquire Clancy from the Senators. The Maple Leafs' board of trustees gave Smythe a budget of $25,000 for Clancy—$10,000 short of Ottawa's exorbitant asking price.

As fate would have it, Smythe had purchased a racehorse named Rare Jewel in 1929. A year later, he entered Rare Jewel in a stakes race. It was a prohibitive long shot at 106-1, but Rare Jewel won. The prize purse, along with Smythe's bet on his horse, was enough to close the deal for Clancy.

Befitting of such a story, it would be the only race Rare Jewel ever won. But it was good enough for Smythe, whose Maple Leafs were now poised to win their first NHL championship since 1922.

Through the Thirties

The Great Depression took its toll on the NHL in the 1930s, as some clubs relocated and ultimately folded. By 1942, the League had contracted to just six teams: Toronto Maple Leafs, Montreal Canadiens, Boston Bruins, New York Rangers, Chicago Blackhawks, and Detroit Red Wings. Nonetheless, fan interest remained strong.

1

Rule changes that were put in place during the 1929–30 season to improve offensive play in the NHL had a profound effect on the sport. The League had averaged less than three goals per game in 1928–29, but it rose to 6.9 through the first third of the following season when the league began allowing the forward pass in all zones.

Players got in the habit of hanging in front of the goal waiting for the puck to arrive. This led to a new offside rule preventing players from entering the opponent's zone before the puck. Still, the combination of changes had a positive impact on scoring. In fact, three players finished the season with more than 40 goals—Cooney Weiland, Dit Clapper and Howie Morenz. Prior to that, no player had scored 40 goals in a season since Joe Malone in the NHL's inaugural season of 1917–18!

The NHL's big names were taking center stage, as the new decade began. The electrifying Morenz led the Montreal Candiens to Stanley Cup titles in 1929–30 and 1930–31. A year later, the Maple Leafs' Ace Bailey, King Clancy

and five-time NHL scoring leader Charlie Conacher helped Conn Smythe fulfill his promise of bringing the Stanley Cup back to Toronto for the first time in 10 years.

However, the Great Depression that began with the stock market crash of 1929 was starting to take its toll. At the start of the 1932–33 season, the NHL implemented its first salary cap. Rosters were reduced to 13 players per team and the payroll was set at $70,000. The maximum player salary was $7,500 so stars, such as Morenz and Eddie Shore, were forced to take pay cuts.

Worse still, some teams couldn't handle the financial troubles. Pittsburgh's steel industry was hit hard by the stock market crash, so the team became the Philadelphia Quakers for the 1930–31 season, but was gone after that year. In 1934, the Senators moved to St. Louis where the franchise died.

The Montreal Maroons won the Stanley Cup in 1934–35, but that success did not guarantee the club financial stability. With the prospects of war in Europe on the horizon, Maroons management withdrew its team from the league after a

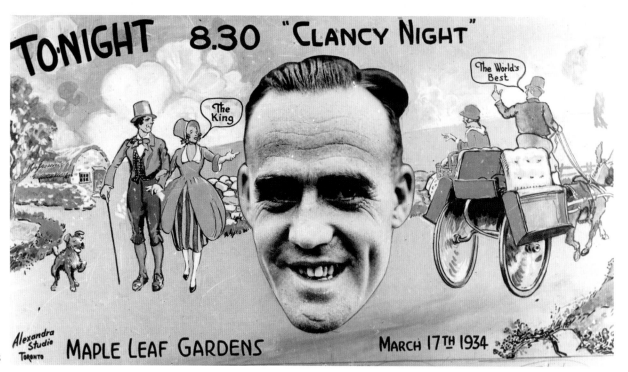

2

3

1: Boston defenseman Eddie Shore won the Hart Trophy four times between 1933 and 1938.

2: Commemorative puck presented to Toronto captain Clarence "Happy" Day after the team's first Stanley Cup championship as Maple Leafs in 1932.

3: The Toronto Maple Leafs often used artwork such as this to hype big games in the 1930s.

4: Montreal Maroons sweater worn by Lionel Conacher in 1936–37.

dismal 1937–38 campaign. With three teams gone, the NHL ended its two-division format in 1938–39.

One team that was not struggling at that time was the franchise in Detroit formerly known as the Falcons. A Chicago grain merchant, James Norris—who, years earlier, had played for the Montreal Hockey Club, nicknamed the Winged Wheelers—bought the Falcons in 1932. Norris

promptly changed the name to the Red Wings in honor of his old squad, and even designed the team's first logo (it appears very similar to the one used today).

The Red Wings, who had never been to the Stanley Cup Final to that point, showed swift improvement. They lost in the Final to the Maroons in 1934, then won back-to-back titles in 1936 and '37.

On their way to the first of those titles, Detroit won what is still the longest game in NHL history. In Game 1 of the semifinals against the Maroons, rookie Modere "Mud" Bruneteau scored in the sixth overtime to give Detroit a 1–0 victory. The game lasted 176 minutes and 30 seconds.

A year after Detroit's back-to-back titles, the NHL saw one of its most improbable champions emerge. The 1937–38 Chicago Blackhawks were in the second year of a grand plan conjured up by team president Major Frederic McLaughlin. The Major's wish was simple: he wanted to field a team of all U.S.-born players.

Almost the entire pool of NHL players at the time were from Canada, so the idea was laughed at throughout the league. Not only were those Americans recruited to play for the Blackhawks late in the 1936–37 season treated harshly by opponents, but also they had a tough time winning over their own Canadian teammates.

Still, McLaughlin was undaunted—and he took his plan to the next level heading into the 1937–38 season. He hired the first American-born coach in former baseball umpire-turned-hockey referee, Bill Stewart. With the likes of goalie Mike Karakas and left winger "Doc" Romnes, Chicago finished third in the American Division, an impressive accomplishment alone. But, when they made it through the playoffs, and defeated the Maple Leafs to capture the Stanley Cup, it was considered near miraculous.

While the all-American Blackhawks were making history, however, the New York Americans were struggling. Hoping to forge a new identity, the club became the Brooklyn Americans in 1941–42, but they were gone from hockey after that season, leaving the NHL with only six teams: the Canadiens, Maple Leafs, Bruins, Blackhawks, Rangers and Red Wings.

Early All-Star Games

Because of the long-running feud between Maple Leafs boss Conn Smythe and Art Ross of the Bruins, games between Toronto and Boston were always rough. The night of December 12, 1933, was rougher than most. Bruins star Eddie Shore blindsided Ace Bailey with a hit from behind that left the Leafs player with a fractured skull. It was ten days before doctors were sure that Bailey would even live, but his hockey career was over. On February 14, 1934, the NHL staged an All-Star Game to aid Bailey and his family. More than $20,000 was raised.

Two later All-Star Games were also held as fundraisers. In November 1937, a game was played to raise money for the family after the death of Howie Morenz. In late October 1939 an NHL All-Star benefit raised money for the family of Babe Siebert, who had drowned the previous August. The first official NHL All-Star Game was held in 1947.

The War Years

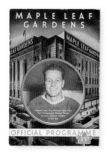

Britain went to war with Germany in September 1939. Since the NHL was populated almost entirely by Canadians it meant that players were called up for military duty long before Pearl Harbor in December 1941. Times were tough, but the NHL adapted—and provided a welcome distraction in wartime.

1

*T*he era of the NHL's "Original Six," which ran from 1942–43 until 1966–67, has been called the golden age of professional hockey. The six teams—the Boston Bruins, Chicago Blackhawks, Detroit Red Wings, Toronto Maple Leafs, New York Rangers and Montreal Canadiens—that battled during these 25 years were "original" in the sense that they preceded the expansion teams of 1967–68. But the "Original Six" were original in more ways than that, as the game changed considerably during this quarter century. The introduction of the center ice red line in 1943–44 made the game faster, while the 1950s and '60s ushered in the slap shot and the functional goaltender's mask. The NHL was creating a modern game with modern heroes.

The league was an exclusive enterprise in those days. Only about 100 players had steady jobs, and it was hardest of all to break in as a goaltender (until 1965–66 teams carried only one). With the advent of the 70-game schedule in 1949–50, teams faced each other 14 times during the regular season, and this familiarity often bred contempt. Grudges were honed and vengeance regularly sought. Many players enjoyed long careers—15 or even 20 seasons—so feuds would be carried on over several seasons.

Still, the dawn of the six-team era was a difficult time for the NHL. Although war had broken out in Europe in September of 1939, the NHL decided to continue operations for the 1939–40 season with as

few disruptions as possible. It wasn't until the 1941–42 campaign that the war truly began to take its toll on the NHL. Boston especially was devastated when the entire "Kraut Line" of Woody Dumart, Milt Schmidt and Bobby Bauer was called up for military service in February 1942. The

2

Major Conn Smythe

Conn Smythe purchased the Toronto St. Patricks on February 14, 1927, and renamed the team the Toronto Maple Leafs. He chose the Maple Leaf name and emblem as a patriotic gesture because it had been the symbol of Canadian soldiers during World War I. Smythe had won the Military Cross as a soldier, and later transferred to the Royal Flying Corps.

Smythe first came to prominence in hockey at the University of Toronto, and was hired to build the New York Rangers in 1926 before being replaced by Lester Patrick. He then built the Maple Leafs into a powerhouse, but after World War II began, Smythe took a leave of absence from hockey operations to recruit a Sportsmen's Battery. He took it overseas, insisted on seeing combat duty himself and was badly wounded in July, 1944. He recovered, and was running the Maple Leafs again by 1945. Smythe remained in charge of the Maple Leafs until retiring in 1961.

3

once-powerful Rangers fell on hard times too, weakened by the loss of six first-string players to the armed forces. (Lester Patrick had to be talked out of suspending the franchise until the war ended.) In Toronto, Conn Smythe prepared to turn over the reins of the Leafs to his colleague Frank Selke while he went to war as leader of a battalion.

Reduced to six franchises for 1942–43, the NHL continued operations with the blessing of the Canadian government, which saw hockey as a distraction from the pressures of the war abroad. However, enlistments and military call-ups had put some 80 NHL players in the armed services, leaving gaping holes in line-ups throughout the league. Acknowledging wartime travel restrictions, overtime was eliminated in regular-season play so that overnight trains would not have to wait for teams to finish games that went into overtime. (Overtime would not return to the regular season until the 1983–84 season.)

To cope with the wartime player shortages, the league cut rosters to 13 skaters plus a goalie, but all of the NHL's clubs were forced to make do with veterans who were past their prime or with youngsters who hadn't gained the usual minor-league seasoning. There were, of course, bright spots among the replacements. Maurice Richard made his

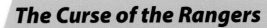

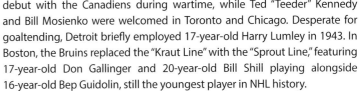

New York Rangers Professional Hockey Club

The Curse of the Rangers

The New York Rangers' Stanley Cup victory in 1940 was the team's third in just their 14th season. It would be 54 years before they'd win another. So, what happened?

Then as now, the Rangers were owned by Madison Square Garden. During the 1940–41 season, the bank loan to build the Garden was paid off and the mortgage was burned in the Stanley Cup bowl. According to legend, this act angered the hockey gods. Another story claims that Red Dutton, who ran the New York Americans, blamed the Rangers for his team's troubles and cursed them when the Americans were forced to suspend operations.

In reality, the Rangers roster was simply decimated by armed forces enlistments in World War II. The team lost its momentum in wartime and did not fully recover until after the 1967 expansion. Then again, it still took another 27 years after that until they finally won again in 1994!

debut with the Canadiens during wartime, while Ted "Teeder" Kennedy and Bill Mosienko were welcomed in Toronto and Chicago. Desperate for goaltending, Detroit briefly employed 17-year-old Harry Lumley in 1943. In Boston, the Bruins replaced the "Kraut Line" with the "Sprout Line," featuring 17-year-old Don Gallinger and 20-year-old Bill Shill playing alongside 16-year-old Bep Guidolin, still the youngest player in NHL history.

At the beginning of the 1943–44 season, the center-ice red line was introduced to speed up play and reduce offside violations. Before the red-line rule, a team coming out of its defensive zone could not pass the puck forward across its own blue line. The new rule allowed a team coming out of its own end to pass the puck right up to center ice, greatly enhancing its ability to clear its own zone and launch an attack. (It would take until the 2005–06 season to allow players to pass the puck from their own zone past the center red line.)

The addition of the center-ice red line was tailor-made for the fast-skating team that Dick Irvin was building in Montreal. The Canadiens freewheeling "Punch Line" of Maurice Richard, Toe Blake, and Elmer Lach would take advantage of the innovation and remain one of the NHL's top forward units for the next five seasons.

Overall, the caliber of play in the NHL definitely deteriorated during the War years, but fans didn't seem to mind. Arenas were filled to capacity most nights, and players were scoring in record numbers. The major on-ice event of the 1944–45 season was the performance of Maurice Richard, whose goal-scoring pace led many to compare him to the late Howie Morenz. Known as the "Rocket," Richard was already earning a reputation for scoring big goals and he tallied 50 times in 50 games that year. Until that season, no player had reached even the 40-goal plateau since Cooney Weiland, Dit Clapper and Howie Morenz did so in 1929–30.

1: Jack Fox (also known as John Fox) was a Maple Leafs prospect with the Syracuse Stars before giving his life in World War II.

2: The Boston Bruins' Kraut Line of Bobby Bauer, Woody Dumart and Milt Schmidt.

3: Red Wings goalie Harry Lumley fends off a Toronto rush ... with help from Ted Lindsay and Gordie Howe. Lumley made his NHL debut at age 17.

4: Montreal Canadiens legend Maurice Richard became the NHL's first 50-goal scorer in 1944–45.

4

Chapter 3
The Modern Era

For a quarter-century, the NHL's Original Six were completely dominated by the "triumphant three," as the Montreal Canadiens, Toronto Maple Leafs, and Detroit Red Wings each became dynasties. The NHL thrived and as the league gradually expanded to become 18 teams, it turned out there was enough talent to fill all those new rosters and keep competition at a high level. Then, when European players came on the scene, the game continued to evolve.

The first team from a southern US state was the Atlanta Flames, which entered the NHL in 1972.

Post-War Dynasties

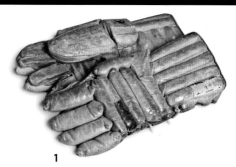

In 25 seasons from 1942–43 to 1966–67, the NHL was dominated by just three teams. The Toronto Maple Leafs, Detroit Red Wings and Montreal Canadiens combined to win the Stanley Cup 24 times! The Canadiens won a record five in a row from 1956 to 1960.

1

With the end of World War II, the NHL—like the rest of North American society—began a period of unprecedented prosperity. This was the age of the Post-War Dynasties, launched by the Toronto Maple Leafs, who won the Stanley Cup four times in five seasons between 1946–47 and 1950–51.

Coached by former captain Hap Day, the Leafs played a rugged two-way game and enjoyed superb clutch goaltending from Turk Broda. Tenacious Teeder Kennedy led the offense, while the defense boasted Gus Mortson, Jimmy Watson and Bill Barilko. None were much of a threat with the puck, though Barilko's overtime goal to win the 1951 Stanley Cup is one of the most famous in hockey history. Barilko died in a plane crash while on a fishing trip that summer, and the Maple Leafs did not win the Cup again until 1962, the year his remains were finally discovered.

In the 25 seasons from 1942–43 to 1966–67, the Rangers, Bruins and Blackhawks struggled annually just to make the playoffs, while Detroit (five), Toronto (nine) and Montreal (10) won the Stanley Cup 24 times! The Red Wings and the Canadiens were the class of the League through the 1950s. In Detroit, general manager Jack Adams and coach Tommy Ivan created one of the greatest teams in NHL history. Their goalie was Terry Sawchuk and the defense featured Red Kelly and Marcel Pronovost.

Gordie Howe

Of all the outstanding players to grace the NHL since its inception, only one made such a lasting impact that he earned the nickname "Mr. Hockey." That was Gordie Howe.

Born in Saskatchewan on March 31, 1928, Howe made his NHL debut for the Detroit Red Wings in 1946 at age 18. He scored a goal in that first game, and he kept on scoring for 26 NHL seasons and retired as the league's all-time leader in goals (801) and points (1,049).

He still owns several other records, including most games played (1,767), most All-Star appearances (23) and most consecutive seasons with at least 20 goals (22). Howe led the Red Wings to four Stanley Cup titles between 1949–50 and 1954–55.

He originally retired in 1971, but two seasons later he signed with the Houston Aeros of the World Hockey Association—where he teamed with his sons, Mark and Marty. Howe played seven seasons in the WHA with the Aeros and Hartford Whalers. When the Whalers joined the NHL for the 1979–80 season, he played his final season in the NHL—at age 52. When Howe died, on June 10, 2016, Gretzky called him "the greatest hockey player ever."

1: Gloves worn by Gordie Howe during the 1952–53 season.

2: Maple Leafs captain Syl Apps, surrounded by owner Conn Smythe (left) and coach Hap Day.

3: Detroit captain Ted Lindsay kisses the Stanley Cup while celebrating with his Red Wings teammates.

2

3

Maurice Richard

Nicknamed "The Rocket" because of his power and intensity, Maurice Richard was the heart and soul of the Montreal Canadiens for 18 seasons and the idol of hockey fans throughout Quebec. Richard was the first player in NHL history to score 50 goals in a season and the first to score 500 in his career. He was named to the NHL All-Star Team 14 years in a row from 1943–44 until 1956–57, including eight selections to the First Team. He played on eight Stanley Cup Championship teams, including five in a row from 1955–56 to 1959–60, and though he never led the league in points, he was the NHL's top goal scorer five times.

Richard's 26 games with three or more goals were the most in the NHL's six-team era. He was also the most prolific playoff scorer of his day with 82 goals, and his record of six career playoff overtime goals stood until 2006. After his death on May 27, 2000, Richard's massive Montreal funeral was broadcast live across Canada.

Offensive stars included the famed and feared "Production Line" of Ted Lindsay, Gordie Howe and Sid Abel. Detroit won seven straight regular season titles from 1948–49 to 1954–55, appeared in seven finals between 1948 and 1956, and won the Stanley Cup four times.

The Canadiens appeared in 10 consecutive finals from 1950–51 to 1959–60, winning the Stanley Cup six times, including five in a row to cap their run. The Canadiens' main star was Maurice "Rocket" Richard, whose ferocious temper regularly got him into trouble. An outburst during a game in Boston on March 13, 1955, became more famous than any goal the Rocket scored. In the midst of a brawl with Bruins defenseman Hal Laycoe, Richard landed two punches in the face of a linesman. NHL president Clarence Campbell suspended him for the rest of the season and the playoffs. When Campbell appeared at the Montreal Forum to watch

the Canadiens—sans Richard—on March 17, the fans rioted and went on a destructive tear through Montreal.

After the Canadiens lost the 1955 Final to Detroit, general manager Frank Selke replaced coach Dick Irvin with Toe Blake. As a former linemate of Richard's, Selke figured Blake would do a better job of reining in the Rocket's temper. The result was the streak of five consecutive Cup wins, and eight in the 13 seasons Blake ran the Canadiens bench. Among the other standouts of the Montreal dynasty were goaltender Jacques Plante; center Jean Beliveau; the Rocket's younger brother, Henri, who joined the team in 1955 and retired in 1975 with a record 11 Cup wins; scoring stars Dickie Moore and Bernie "Boom Boom" Geoffrion, who popularized the use of the slap shot; and defenseman Doug Harvey.

By the early 1960s, the Maple Leafs were again ready to challenge for the Stanley Cup. Punch Imlach's Toronto teams were the NHL's first truly engineered dynasty. Imlach retained established players like George Armstrong, Tim Horton and Frank Mahovlich, added talent from the farm system such as Carl Brewer, Dave Keon and Bob Pulford, but also he stirred in veterans from other teams—Bert Olmstead from Montreal; Allan Stanley from Boston; Red Kelly, Terry Sawchuk, and Marcel Pronovost from Detroit; Ed Litzenberger from Chicago; and Andy Bathgate from New York. The results were Stanley Cup wins in 1962, 1963, 1964, and 1967.

When the NHL doubled in size for the 1967–68 season, many good players who had been languishing in the minors finally got their chance. Yet to this day the players who had excelled during the league's second quarter century from 1942 to 1967 are remembered with a particular reverence and affection.

5

4

4: Maple Leafs jersey worn by Red Kelly during the 1967 Stanley Cup Final.

5: Goalie Jacques Plante helped the Canadiens win the Stanley Cup a record five years in a row from 1956 to 1960.

6: Dave Keon, MVP of the 1967 playoffs, takes a celebratory drink from the Stanley Cup.

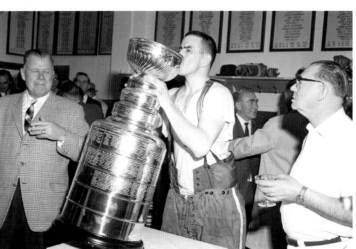

6

From Six to 12 to 18

The NHL doubled in size from six to 12 teams for the 1967–68 season, including two franchises on the West Coast. Six years later, the League expanded again, and then numbered 18 teams. Despite some growing pains, expansion paved the way for new stars and new audiences.

One of the earliest notions that the NHL might grow beyond six teams came in May of 1952. Jim Hendy, general manager of the American Hockey League's Cleveland Barons, believed his club was about to become the NHL's seventh member. It had taken six months of lobbying to reach this point, and one Cleveland sports columnist went so far as to write, "Our city has been awarded a franchise in the NHL." However, two months later, the Barons' application was denied over worries that the ownership lacked sufficient working capital.

Talk of expansion heated up again later in the 1950s once air travel began to provide easier transport across the continent. Major League Baseball saw the Dodgers and the Giants leave New York City for Los Angeles and San Francisco in 1958 then began adding expansion teams in 1961 and 1962. The American Football League set up shop alongside the National Football League in 1960. In 1962, legendary sports columnist Jim Murray of the *Los Angeles Times* wrote: "The National Hockey League makes a mockery of its title by restricting its franchises to six teams." Minor league hockey was already beginning to expand across the United States.

Finally, on March 11, 1965, the NHL announced expansion plans. It would begin evaluating applications from responsible groups to create a second six-team division. Official acceptance on February 8, 1966 found Los Angeles, San Francisco (Oakland), St. Louis, Pittsburgh, Philadelphia and Minneapolis–St. Paul as the representatives of the new division. Applications from Buffalo, Baltimore and Vancouver were rejected. The cost of a new franchise was $2 million. On June 6, 1967, an Expansion Draft was held in Montreal. The Los Angeles Kings, Oakland Seals, St Louis Blues, Pittsburgh Penguins, Philadelphia Flyers and Minnesota North Stars were each allowed to choose 20 players from a pool of unprotected "Original Six" talent.

The 12-team NHL was aligned with an East and a West Division for the 1967–68 season, with the expansion clubs all playing in the West. The first four teams in each division qualified for the playoffs, which now consisted of three best-of-seven rounds. The quarterfinals and semifinals would determine the champion of each division, with the two division winners meeting in the finals. This guaranteed that an expansion club would meet an established team for the Stanley Cup.

1: Magazines like *Hockey Pictorial* had a lot more territory to cover starting in 1967.

2: Red Berenson of the St. Louis Blues.

3: Islanders captain Denis Potvin carries the Stanley Cup with Butch Goring right behind him.

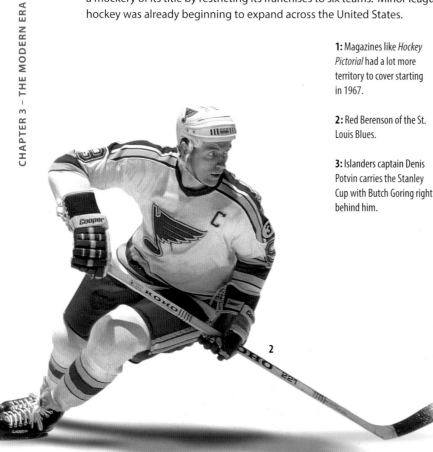

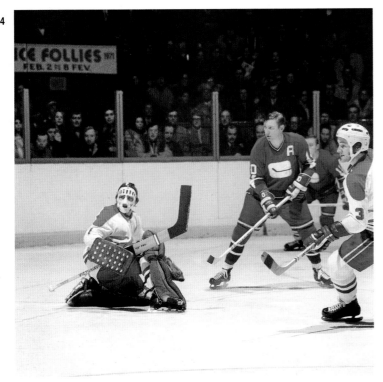

4

5

4: Canadiens goalie Rogie Vachon and defenseman J.C. Tremblay fend off Ray Cullen of the Vancouver Canucks.

5: Randy Manery, Daniel Bouchard and Pat Ribble of the Atlanta Flames with Guy Lafleur of the Canadiens.

6: A pocket schedule for the first season of the Kansas City Scouts.

As it turned out, players like Terry Crisp, Gary Dornhoefer, Bill Goldsworthy, and others whom NHL teams had buried in the minors or restricted to part-time duty actually had the skills to compete. Philadelphia ended the season on top of the West Division with 73 points, one ahead of Los Angeles, three ahead of St. Louis, and four up on Minnesota. Just six points separated the Flyers from the fifth-place Penguins. The West Division's top scorer was Minnesota's Wayne Connelly, who had 35 goals including a league-leading 14 scored on the power-play. (The Blues' Red Berenson would become the first expansion player to crack the top 10 in scoring with 82 points in 1968–69.) In the playoffs, St. Louis proved there was no substitute for experience—and a few ex-Canadiens in the line-up. Dickie Moore, Doug Harvey, Jacques Plante and Red Berenson led the Blues to the Stanley Cup Final. Once there, the Canadiens swept them, but each game was decided by only one goal.

So successful was the first expansion that another followed in the fall of 1970. Vancouver and Buffalo made their respective debuts in the NHL following a realignment of divisions. (Chicago moved to the West Division while the two new entries joined the East.) Meanwhile, other cities clamored for admittance to the NHL. In an interview during the 1970–71 season, New York Rangers governor William Jennings said he expected Atlanta and Long Island (New York) to become potential expansion applicants by 1974. However, when the World Hockey Association revealed plans to open as a rival league in 1972, the NHL quickly admitted the New York Islanders and Atlanta Flames for the 1972–73 season. Two years later, the NHL grew to 18 franchises with the admission of the Washington Capitals and the Kansas City Scouts. Expansion fees for the six teams that entered the NHL in the 1970s had grown to $6 million.

In the spring of 1974, the Philadelphia Flyers became Stanley Cup champions in just their seventh season. In 1980, the New York Islanders won the Stanley Cup in their eighth year. But other expansion teams struggled. The Oakland Seals moved to Cleveland in 1976, but lasted just two seasons there, while the Flames didn't find success until moving to Calgary in 1980. The Scouts lasted just two years in Kansas City, then spent six seasons as the Colorado Rockies before becoming the New Jersey Devils in 1982. Even in hockey-mad Minnesota, the North Stars became the Dallas Stars in 1993. However, later expansion in the 1990s would see the NHL return to almost every market it had looked to originally as the league grew to 30 teams.

6

Bobby Hull

When Bobby Hull joined the Chicago Blackhawks as an 18-year-old in 1957–58, the team had missed the playoffs for 11 of 12 seasons. Attendance was dismal and the franchise had been in danger of folding. Hull's scoring exploits attracted huge crowds to the Chicago Stadium, and by 1961, the Blackhawks were Stanley Cup champions.

Hull was muscular with a booming slap shot that was powerful and accurate. He was also the fastest skater in the game. Combining those facts with his blonde, good looks, Hull was nicknamed "The Golden Jet." He led the league in goals on seven occasions and won the Art Ross Trophy three times. In 1961–62 he became just the third player in NHL history to score 50 goals in a season, and he pushed the single-season mark to 58 in 1968–69. Hull gave instant credibility to the World Hockey Association in 1972 when he signed a 10-year deal worth $2.75 million with the Winnipeg Jets.

Power Hockey in the 1970s

1

Scoring soared as the National Hockey League expanded. So did the mayhem on the ice, as the tough Boston Bruins and Philadelphia Flyers teams won championships, but the dominant team of the decade was the Montreal Canadiens who combined toughness with finesse.

In a sense, the 1970s really include the first three seasons of NHL expansion, starting in 1967–68. The Toronto Maple Leafs had upset the Montreal Canadiens to close out the "Original Six" era in 1967, but the Canadiens bounced back to win the Stanley Cup in the first two years of hockey's new age.

The Canadiens were rapidly aging in places—Jean Beliveau and Henri Richard were keys at center, and the venerable Gump Worsley split time in goal—but were youthful in others. Brilliant general manager Sam Pollock moved veterans in and out to keep the team fresh and strong. The younger athletes—Jacques Lemaire, Yvan Cournoyer, Peter Mahovlich, and Ken Dryden—moved to the forefront as the Habs took the Cup again in both 1971 and 1973. But the best was yet to come, as Montreal would later stake out a new Cup dynasty and establish themselves as the team of the 1970s.

In Boston, where the Bruins had been NHL strugglers since the 1940s, the franchise's fortunes improved around two key moves as expansion dawned: signing Bobby Orr, and gaining Phil Esposito from Chicago in a six-player trade. Both proceeded to rewrite the record book while galvanizing a team that earned a reputation as "The Big Bad Bruins." They were a sneering, black-garbed hit squad of tough hockey talent that

seemed to run up six or seven goals every night. Boston won the Cup in 1970 and 1972, and reached the Final again in the 1974, 1977 and 1978.

The Rangers had last won it all in 1940 and since then had been even weaker than Boston. But, like the Bruins, the Rangers began building when expansion arrived. By the early 1970s they had assembled a swift, clean, skillful side able to contend for the Cup. Those Ranger teams featured the slick forward line of Jean Ratelle, Rod Gilbert and Vic Hadfield, young

3

1: Bobby Orr was a Blackhawk when he hawked a Bally pinball machine.

2: The Toronto Maple Leafs' Stanley Cup parade in 1967 marked the end of the Original Six era.

3: Philadelphia teammates (from left) Bernie Parent, Bobby Clarke and Bill Clement accept the Stanley Cup from NHL president Clarence Campbell.

4: Stan Mikita of the Chicago Black Hawks skates on the ice against the Minnesota North Stars at the Metropolitan Sports Center in Bloomington, Minnesota.

2

4

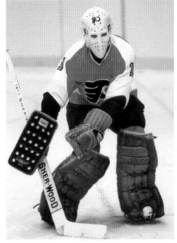

5: Montreal's Yvon Lambert, Yvan Cournoyer and Guy Lafleur celebrate with the Stanley Cup in 1976.

6: Bernie Parent, goalkeeper for the Philadelphia Flyers, in action.

7: Ken Dryden helped the Montreal Canadiens win the Stanley Cup six times in the 1970s.

8: Stan Mikita model helmet worn by Toronto's Ron Ellis

defenseman Brad Park and the great goaltending of Eddie Giacomin and Gilles Villemure.

Although they were on the wrong end of the Phil Esposito deal, Chicago still had superstars like Bobby Hull and Stan Mikita leading a team that had been strong throughout the 1960s. They got a further boost when the NHL added two more expansion teams in 1970 and moved the Blackhawks into the West Division. With Tony Esposito in net, Chicago won the division easily for the next three years, and went through to the Stanley Cup Final in 1971 and 1973.

The rival World Hockey Association began play in 1972–73, enticing Bobby Hull and several other big names to jump from the NHL and hiking the average player salary in both leagues. With as many as 32 teams in the NHL and WHA combined, there wasn't always enough talent to go around, meaning Montreal could finish atop the NHL with 120 points in 1972–73 while the New York Islanders finished last with just 30. In 1974–75, the Canadiens, Kings, Sabres and Flyers all topped 100 points, but the Washington Capitals managed only 21 on a record of 8–67–5.

By the middle of the 1970s, the Philadelphia Flyers had proved to be the most successful of the NHL expansion teams—and also the most notorious. A decent side in their first few NHL campaigns, the Flyers opted to get much tougher and won through intimidation as much as skill. Alongside their tough guys and plumbers, the Flyers had an elegant forward in Rick MacLeish as well as an effective first line in Bill Barber, Bobby Clarke and Reggie Leach. They also had Bernie Parent in the net. The Flyers won four straight division titles and consecutive Stanley Cup championships in 1974 and 1975 and forced many teams to adopt elements of their aggressive style.

One team eschewed the more aggressive style of the NHL in the 1970s. The Montreal Canadiens returned as conquering heroes in 1976, paragons of the best hockey had to offer. Guy Lafleur had blossomed into the game's most electrifying scorer, Steve Shutt proved a capable sniper on the opposite wing, checking forward Bob Gainey turned into a force of nature at playoff time, and Serge Savard, Larry Robinson, and

Guy Lapointe—the "Big Three"—numbered among the best defensemen in the game.

In 1975–76, Montreal breezed through the regular season and early playoff rounds to face the defending champion Flyers for the Stanley Cup. In this showdown of hockey philosophies, the Canadiens swept Philadelphia in four straight games. Montreal rarely took a night off for the rest of the decade. In the 1976–77 season, the Canadiens set records with 60 wins and 132 points, and then repeated in the Final with a four-game sweep of Boston. Two more regular-season cakewalks ended with championships as the Canadiens ran their Stanley Cup streak to four straight seasons through 1978–79. The Islanders and Oilers—dynasties that followed the Canadiens in the 1980s—both used aspects of the Canadiens system as models for their own success.

Phil Esposito

With size and strength that made it difficult for defensemen to clear him out from in front of the net, Phil Esposito became a scoring superstar with the Boston Bruins. After finishing the 1967–68 season as runner-up in scoring behind former Chicago teammate Stan Mikita, the burly Bruin became the first player in NHL history to reach 100 points in 1968–69 en route to winning both the Art Ross and Hart trophies. In 1970–71, the Boston star smashed Bobby Hull's single-season record of 58 goals with 76. He also collected 76 assists for 152 points. By 1973–74, Phil Esposito had won the Art Ross Trophy five times and the Hart as MVP twice.

Traded to New York in a stunning deal in 1975, Esposito led the Rangers in scoring four years in a row and helped them reach the Stanley Cup Final in 1979. When he retired in 1981, Esposito's 717 goals and 1,590 points trailed only Gordie Howe's totals of 801 and 1,850 in the NHL record book.

The First European Invasion

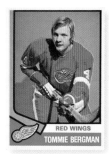

Increased exposure to international hockey began to change ideas about how the game could be played. Europeans started to enter the NHL in the early 1970s. Sweden's Borje Salming became a star with the Toronto Maple Leafs and helped pave the way for an influx of new talent.

1

Hockey in North America had gotten bigger, but had it gotten any better? The NHL of the late 1960s and early 1970s was not very different than it had been in the years immediately following World War II. The game still moved in straight lines. All the emphasis was on the puck carrier, the other four skaters waiting, unthreatening and non-creative. Demographics had not changed much either. The league was almost entirely Canadian. When Tommy Williams joined the Boston Bruins during the 1961–62 season, he became the first American to play regularly in the NHL since Frank Brimsek retired in 1950. Sweden's Ulf Sterner played four games for the New York Rangers in 1964–65, and Czech native Jaroslav Jirik played three games for St. Louis in 1969–70. Then 1972 changed everything.

The impact of 1972 Canada–Soviet Summit Series was felt at many levels. It established international hockey involving the NHL and the Soviet Union as a first-rank attraction. It also demonstrated that the best hockey played in Europe was on a par with that of the NHL and that precision passing and high-speed play executed by superbly conditioned athletes were tough to beat. EuroSoviet hockey was a revelation with its swirling, cycling, criss-crossing patterns of attack and emphasis on skating and passing. The Soviets couldn't leave their country to play here, but other Europeans could. Sweden's Thommie Bergman joined the Detroit Red Wings for the 1972–73 season, and the Maple Leafs lured Inge Hammarstrom and Borje Salming to Toronto in 1973–74.

Borje Salming was the first European player to become a star in the NHL. He was forced to endure taunts and physical abuse from opponents in his early years, but he was as smooth, skillful, smart and tough as any NHL defenseman. He starred in the league for 17 seasons and was elected to the Hockey Hall of Fame in 1996. Salming

excelled at blocking shots, and was a strong skater who could rush the puck effectively and set up plays. He established a Maple Leafs record by being named to the NHL All-Star Team for six straight seasons from 1974–75 to 1979–80, and was the runner up to Larry Robinson in Norris Trophy voting in 1976–77 and 1979–80.

4

Hockey cards of three of the earliest Swedes in the NHL:
1: Tommie Bergman, Detroit Red Wings.
2: Borje Salming, Toronto.
3: Inge Hammarstrom, Toronto Maple Leafs.

4: Borje Salming starred with the Toronto Maple Leafs in the 1970s.

5: Ulf Sterner with the New York Rangers.

5

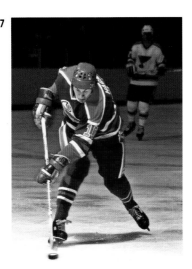

6: Jari Kurri proved a perfect finisher for Wayne Gretzky's slick passes and became one of the NHL's top goal scorers.

7: Fellow Finn Matti Hagman paved the way for his countrymen when he joined the Boston Bruins in 1976–77. Hagman finished his NHL career in 1982—as an Edmonton teammate of Kurri—but continued to play back in Europe for another ten years.

Despite Salming's star power, the NHL was slow to accept European talent. The rival World Hockey Association was much more welcoming. The Winnipeg Jets won WHA championships with an electrifying, largely European roster. Anders Hedberg and Ulf Nilsson were among six new European players who joined the Jets in 1974–75. Hedberg and Nilsson teamed with Bobby Hull to form the most potent forward line in the WHA. Converting Nilsson's slick passes, Hull set a pro hockey record with 77 goals that season. Hedberg had 53 goals and 47 assists and was named WHA rookie of the year. He and Nilsson both topped 100 points in each of the four years they spent in Winnipeg, with Hedberg never scoring fewer than 50 goals. The Swedish superstars both signed two-year contracts worth $1 million with the New York Rangers in 1978–79. Hedberg went on to play seven seasons in the NHL, and though he was unable to match his WHA totals, he never scored fewer than 20 goals in any full season.

In 1976–77, Matti Hagman became the first Finnish player in the NHL when he signed with the Boston Bruins. In 1980–81, he was a member of the Edmonton Oilers, where a young Finnish sniper named Jari Kurri

Hockey cards depicting two of the HLNHL's earliest Swedish superstars:

8: Ulf Nilsson, New York Rangers.

9: Kent-Erik Andersson, Minnesota North Stars.

10: Anders Hedberg and Ulf Nilsson left the Winnepeg Jets of the WHA for the NHL's New York Rangers in 1978–79.

joined him. That same season, Czechoslovakian brothers Peter and Anton Stastny defected to join the Quebec Nordiques. (Brother Marian followed the next year.) Before the start of the 1981–82 season, New York Rangers general manager Craig Patrick named his former boss Herb Brooks from the 1980 U.S. Olympic team as the Rangers head coach. Brooks instituted a crowd-pleasing European-style offense that was built around weaving, criss-crossing, and circling. The Rangers couldn't do a whole lot with it, but the Edmonton Oilers merged traditional NHL tactics with modern European methods to great success. The Edmonton style combined North American strength with European speed, and, of course, the wizardry of Wayne Gretzky.

Gretzky's skill as a playmaker required a reason to pass and someone to pass to. This pushed teammates like Kurri, Paul Coffey, Mark Messier and Glenn Anderson to think ahead, to create and find open ice in order to receive Gretzky's passes. Open ice is rarely found at the end of a straight-ahead dash, but across the width of the ice where there is more space, so that's where the Oilers went.

This new, European-influenced, passing game made the player without the puck more important than the player with it. He was quicker, more creative and maneuverable, and this meant—obviously—he was the more dangerous one. The old hockey passing patterns, with their rugby roots, were finally dead.

Vladislav Tretiak

Vladislav Tretiak was the greatest goaltender ever produced by the Soviet Union. He joined the roster of Moscow's Central Red Army team at 17 in 1968–69, and was a member of 13 Soviet League champions over the next 15 years.

Tretiak came to the attention of North American fans with his brilliant play during the 1972 Summit Series. On New Year's Eve in 1975, he helped his Red Army team earn a 3–3 tie with the Montreal Canadiens despite being outshot 38–13 in one of the greatest games ever played. He was named MVP when the Soviets won the Canada Cup in 1981. When he retired after the 1983–84 season, Tretiak had won 10 World Championships with the Soviet national team and three Olympic gold medals.

In 98 World Championship games, he had a goals-against average of 1.92. He had a 1.74 mark in 19 Olympic Games matches. In 1989, he became the first Soviet-trained player elected to the Hockey Hall of Fame.

Chapter 4
The Gretzky Era

From child prodigy to superstar, Wayne Gretzky's nickname of "The Great One" was an understatement—"Greatest One" is more appropriate. Gretzky re-wrote the record books with his scoring prowess, and he became such a popular figure in American sports that the NHL was able to expand into new markets. By the end of the 20th century, the NHL was truly an international product and Gretzky had much to do with its popularity.

Wayne Gretzky rewrote the record books
and no one has surpassed him.

Growing Up Gretzky

Wayne Gretzky became famous when he scored 378 goals as an 11-year-old in 1971–72. He turned professional in the World Hockey Association at age 17, and began re-writing the National Hockey League record book almost from the time he entered the League at age 18 in 1979–80.

1

*F*ew athletes in any sport have reached the top with as much hype—or as many naysayers—as Wayne Gretzky. Famous from the time he was 10 years old, he turned professional in the World Hockey Association when he was only 17, but Gretzky still had many doubters when he entered the NHL as an 18-year-old. He proved his critics wrong, just as he had every step of the way since learning to skate at the age of two.

The story of the backyard rink at the family home in Brantford, Ontario has become the stuff of legend, but Wayne Gretzky actually learned to skate behind his grandparent's farm on the nearby Nith River. Young Wayne so obviously loved being out on the ice that his father Walter (like so many fathers before and since) built a backyard rink when his son was four.

When Wayne was five, he wanted to play organized hockey. He showed up for a local team (the Nadrofsky Steelers) but, in Brantford, there was no minor hockey before the age of 10. So he continued to practice on the backyard rink. A year later, Wayne went out for the team again. This time, they agreed to let him play. He scored his only goal that year in the team's final game. "It's the only time I ever felt overmatched," he once said of his first season, but his coach recognized his budding talent. A year later, aged seven, Gretzky scored 27 goals playing with his 10-year-old teammates. In 1969–70, he had 104 (plus 63 assists) in 62 games and, in the following season, he had 196 goals and 120 assists in 76 games.

By the time he was 10 in 1971–72 (he turned 11 midway through the season), Gretzky collected 378 goals and 139 assists in 85 games and began to attract attention from the national media. But he was not just a hockey prodigy. He enjoyed lacrosse ("that's where I learned to protect myself from hard body checks") and he loved baseball. "If I couldn't play hockey," he told the *Toronto Telegram* in his first major interview, "I'd like to play baseball with the Oakland A's and Vida Blue."

Skinny, awkward-looking and small for his age, Gretzky nonetheless put up more big numbers as he moved up in age brackets, but he also began to face growing resentment in Brantford.

Teammates always recognized his talent and his work ethic, but parents were often jealous of his ice time. In the summer of 1975, Wayne moved in with a surrogate family in suburban Toronto in order to blend in better at

3

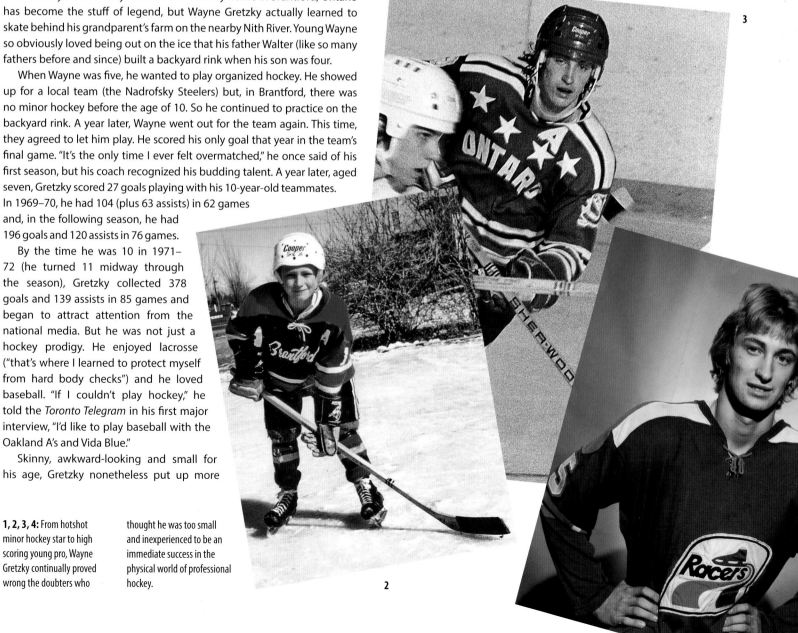

1, 2, 3, 4: From hotshot minor hockey star to high scoring young pro, Wayne Gretzky continually proved wrong the doubters who thought he was too small and inexperienced to be an immediate success in the physical world of professional hockey.

2

Marcel Dionne

In 18 seasons in the NHL, Marcel Dionne ranked among the NHL's top 10 scorers on eight occasions, and he finished as the runner-up for the Art Ross Trophy on three occasions. His one scoring title came in 1979–80 when he tied Wayne Gretzky with 137 points, but outscored him 53 goals to 51. It was one of six 50-goal seasons in Dionne's career, tying him with Guy Lafleur and Mario Lemieux for second all-time. Only Gretzky and Mike Bossy (with nine 50-goal seasons) have ever had more.

Dionne never played on a Stanley Cup winner in his career, but his offensive totals rank him among the best players in NHL history. At the time of his retirement in 1989, his 731 goals trailed only Gordie Howe and his 1,040 assists ranked behind only Howe and Wayne Gretzky. Today, his career total of 1,771 points ranks him fifth NHL history. Dionne was elected to the Hockey Hall of Fame in 1992.

high school and to play more competitive hockey. He was just 14.

After two years in Toronto (and a three-game trial with the Peterborough Petes at age 15), Gretzky joined the Sault Ste. Marie Greyhounds of the Ontario Hockey League in 1977–78. He had long worn number 9 in tribute to his hero Gordie Howe, but that number was already taken with the Greyhounds. He tried 14, then 19 before switching to 99. Though the gangly 16-year-old with the unlikely name and the outlandish number was still seen as a fluke by many, his 70 goals and 182 points in just 64 games ranked him second in the league behind Dino Ciccarelli and Bobby Smith, who were both older and more experienced.

At 17, Gretzky was still too young to sign with an NHL team, but the WHA had no such age restriction. Nelson Skalbania signed Gretzky for the Indianapolis Racers, but sold him to the Edmonton Oilers shortly after the start of the 1978–79 season. Gretzky's 110 points in the WHA still did not silence many critics, who pointed out that he was not playing against the top competition. But soon he would be.

When the Oilers entered the NHL in 1979–80, Gretzky put up 137 points! He tied Marcel Dionne for the scoring title, and though he did not receive the Art Ross Trophy because Dionne had scored more goals (he was also denied the Calder Trophy as best rookie because of his year in the WHA), he did win the Hart Trophy as NHL MVP and the Lady Byng Trophy for sportsmanship. And still there were doubters! They criticized his speed, his

average shot and his herky-jerky style. Yet Gretzky was always a fraction of a second ahead of the play. Since childhood, his father had taught him to head for where the puck was going, not where it had been. Whether through sheer practice or innate talent (probably both), Gretzky's on-ice vision far surpassed anyone's in the game.

Slowly, as the records fell (he scored 92 goals in 1981–82 and pushed the mark for assists and points to 163 and 215), the doubters began to disappear. Finally, when the Stanley Cup titles began to pile up, there was no longer any question. Wayne Gretzky was truly "The Great One."

6

5

5: Marcel Dionne's Los Angeles Kings sweater. Dionne was Gretzky's main scoring rival during his first two NHL seasons.

6: Wayne Gretzky finished his career with

three seasons in New York, but the Rangers could not make it to the Stanley Cup Final.

7: Wayne Gretzky hoisted the Stanley Cup four times with the Edmonton Oilers, in 1984, 1985, 1987 and 1988.

7

Hockey in the 1980s: 99 Time

The NHL had grown to 21 teams and had its first 200-point player. The New York Islanders and Edmonton Oilers dominated the League and would win eight of ten Stanley Cup titles as high-scoring became the name of the game. The League boasted 50-goal scorers and 100-point players in record numbers.

1

When the NHL expanded to take in four former WHA cities in the summer of 1979, it inaugurated a period of stability in which the league would keep its 21-team configuration for 12 seasons.

The Edmonton Oilers, Winnipeg Jets, Quebec Nordiques and Hartford Whalers were allowed to protect only two skaters and one goaltender from their WHA rosters when they entered the NHL in 1979–80. The rights to other players previously drafted by NHL clubs reverted to the NHL

organization that had originally selected them. Mike Liut joined the St. Louis Blues after two seasons with the Cincinnati Stingers and became one of the top goaltenders of the 1980s. The Atlanta Flames reclaimed Kent Nilsson from the Winnipeg Jets and he became a top NHL scorer after the team relocated to Calgary.

The four new NHL franchises restocked their rosters by participating in an expansion draft, acquiring up to 15 skaters and two goaltenders from the established clubs. Several ex-NHLers who had blossomed into stars in the WHA—players such as Blaine Stoughton and Mike Rogers—were either retained or re-acquired by their former WHA clubs. The Edmonton Oilers were able to keep Wayne Gretzky by claiming him as a priority selection.

The four expansion teams also participated in the 1979 Amateur Draft, which, that year, was renamed the "Entry Draft" because of the availability of players with professional (WHA) experience. Former WHA players who had turned pro while still below the NHL's minimum draft age of 18—including Mike Gartner, Rick Vaive, Michel Goulet, and Mark Messier—were among the top players available in what proved to be a strong draft year.

Meantime, a former NHL expansion franchise, the New York Islanders, had quietly built an outstanding hockey team under the guidance of general manager Bill Torrey. The team revolved around defenseman Denis Potvin, forwards Bryan Trottier and

2

3

5

4

1: Jarri Kurri (right) and Wayne Gretzky were teammates at Edmonton and Los Angeles as well as in many All-Star Games.

2: Mario Lemieux ended Wayne Gretzky's lock on the NHL scoring title.

3: Mike Bossy scored 50 goals in 50 games in 1980–81.

4: Right wing Mike Garter scored 708 goals in 19 NHL seasons.

5: A young Mark Messier with the Edmonton Oilers.

6: Rick Vaive was the Maple Leafs' first 50-goal scorer.

7: Battlin' Billy Smith anchored the New York Islanders Dynasty.

8: The 1980s often saw Wayne Gretzky surrounded by silverware.

9: A hockey game based on computer analysis of the 1985-85 season.

Oilers led an offensive revolution throughout the NHL in the 1980s that was boosted by more European players and an improving U.S. college system that put more talented performers into the league than ever before.

Beginning in 1980–81, Wayne Gretzky led the NHL in scoring for seven straight seasons, including a team record-setting 1983–84 campaign that saw the Oilers scored an unprecedented 446 goals (an average of 5.58 per game) while collecting a decade-high 57 wins and 119 points en route to their first Stanley Cup title. Gretzky had 87 goals and 205 points in 74 games, producing 153 of those points during a record 51-game scoring streak that began at the start of the season. Gretzky and teammate Paul Coffey formed a scoring duo reminiscent of Phil Esposito and Bobby Orr. Coffey finished second in league scoring with 40 goals and 86 assists for 126 points, joining Orr as just the second defenseman to score 40 goals in a season. Glenn Anderson added 54 goals, while Jari Kurri scored 52 to give the Oilers three 50-goal scorers in the same season. It's a feat matched only one time in NHL history—by the same three teammates two years later!

Hockey fans of the 1980s were most fortunate indeed. Not only did they have #99 to watch, but #66 as well. Mario Lemieux entered the NHL with a 100-point season in 1984–85 and ended Wayne Gretzky's seven-year hold on the Art Ross Trophy with the first of back-to-back scoring titles in 1987–88. Other stars of hockey's most explosive offensive era included Denis Savard with the Chicago Blackhawks, Bernie Federko with the St. Louis Blues, Neal Broten with the Minnesota North Stars and Dale Hawerchuk with the Winnipeg Jets.

Mike Bossy and goaltender Billy Smith. Like any great hockey team, the Islanders also had a talented supporting cast that included players like Clark Gillies, Bob Nystrom and Butch Goring. The Islanders were never flashy, but they played a tough, disciplined game and made few mistakes. In 1979–80, the Islanders joined the Philadelphia Flyers as the second expansion team to win the Stanley Cup. They went on to win the Cup four years in a row. The Islanders swept Edmonton to win their fourth Cup in 1983, but the Oilers turned the tables on them a year later.

Edmonton general manager Glen Sather had built a very different team than the conservative Islanders. Sather had visited Sweden and Finland when he was coaching the Oilers in the WHA, and he liked what he had seen there. The European style he'd witnessed demanded creativity and Sather knew that in Wayne Gretzky he had the most creative player in NHL history. Sather also needed players who could skate, so the Oilers landed the likes of Jari Kurri, Glenn Anderson and Paul Coffey to join Gretzky and Mark Messier, a tough-as-nails forward with blazing speed. The team also found a great goaltender in Grant Fuhr. And they needed him. The Oilers had a high-octane attack, and though it took more attention to defense to start winning championships, the

Peter Stastny

Peter Stastny (center) and his brothers Anton and Marian were star players in Czechoslovakia during the 1970s. The Quebec Nordiques drafted Anton in 1979, and Peter was signed as a free agent after the two defected to North America. Both made their NHL debuts with the Nordiques in 1980–81. Marian joined them the following year.

All three Stastny brothers made an impact in Quebec, but only Peter became a superstar. He had been player of the year in Czechoslovakia in 1979–80 and followed up by winning the Calder Trophy as rookie of the year in the NHL. Stastny had 100 points or more seven times in his career and was in the top-10 in scoring on six occasions. Only Wayne Gretzky had more points than Stastny during the 1980s. He played in six All-Star games, but in an era dominated by centers such as Gretzky, Marcel Dionne, Bryan Trottier and Mario Lemieux, Stastny never earned postseason all-star honors.

Hockey in the 1990s

Taking its cue from the success of Wayne Gretzky's move to Los Angeles in 1988, the NHL entertained further expansion and grew to 30 teams as the century ended. Many of them were in non-traditional markets in the Sun Belt states of the southern and western U.S.

1

On August 9, 1988, Wayne Gretzky was traded to the Los Angeles Kings. Four other players also changed hands, along with three draft picks, and the Oilers received $15 million. Canadians were stunned, but Gretzky became a glamorous spokesman for the sport in the United States, where someone of his stature was needed to sell the game. Almost overnight, Gretzky made hockey cool in sunny California and some of Hollywood's biggest stars came to see him play.

There is little question that the Gretzky trade precipitated the expansion of the NHL game into new U.S. markets in the 1990s. Franchises soon sprung up in San Jose and Anaheim, Tampa Bay and Miami, while several of the league's northern-based teams relocated to Dallas, Carolina, Phoenix and Colorado. By 2000–01, the NHL had grown from 21 to 30 teams with the addition of the Nashville Predators, Atlanta Thrashers, Columbus Blue Jackets and Minnesota Wild.

The rapid growth of the NHL in the 1990s was fueled, in no small part, by greater access to foreign hockey markets. The league for years had featured a sprinkling of players from Sweden, the Czech Republic and Finland, but the real influx didn't begin until the early 1990s. When Communism

collapsed and the Iron Curtain came down, players from Eastern Europe could come to North America whenever they wanted without having to defect.

Wayne Gretzky continued to be the NHL's dominant presence throughout the 1990s. He won scoring titles with the Kings in 1989–90, 1990–91 and 1993–94 and led Los Angeles to the 1993 Stanley Cup Final, but more and more players around the league were beginning to share the offensive spotlight with him. Mark Messier was already a star in his

3

1: Helmet worn by Wayne Gretzky during his days with the Los Angeles Kings.

2: Wayne Gretzky is introduced to the media in Los Angeles.

3: San Jose's corporately named HP Pavilion.

4: After winning the Stanley Cup twice with the Montreal Canadiens, Patrick Roy won two more as a member of the Colorado Avalanche.

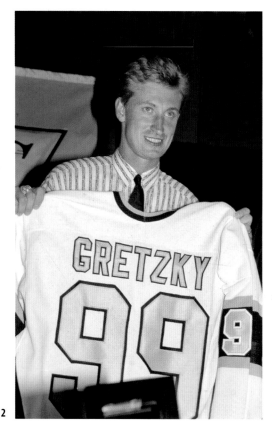

2

4

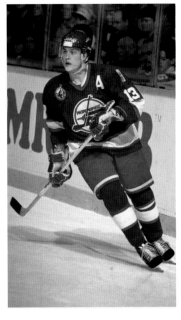

6: Jaromir Jagr formed a potent partnership with Mario Lemieux as they brought the Stanley Cup to Pittsburgh in 1991 and 1992.

7: Teemu Selanne scored 76 goals for the Winnipeg Jets as a rookie in 1992–93.

8: "Super Mario" Lemieux was Gretzky's closest rival for the NHL's best player in the early 1990s until illness struck.

9: Gloves worn by Joe Mullen when he became the first U.S.-born player to score 500 goals.

7

8

own right but he had long played in Gretzky's shadow in Edmonton. Messier captained the Gretzky-less Oilers to their fifth Stanley Cup victory in 1990, then earned himself legendary status in 1994 when he captained the New York Rangers to their first Stanley Cup title in 54 years. But the two biggest offensive stars of the 1990s both played in Pittsburgh.

Mario Lemieux had been the NHL's top draft choice in 1984 and slowly helped the Penguins develop into a top team. Despite battling chronic back problems and then Hodgkin's disease, Lemieux added four scoring titles to the two he had won in the 1980s and led the Penguins to back-to-back Stanley Cup titles in 1991 and 1992. Jaromir Jagr was a rookie on Pittsburgh's first Stanley Cup team and quickly became one of the league's top performers. He became the first European-trained player to win the Art Ross Trophy as NHL scoring champion in 1994–95, and later won four scoring titles in a row from 1997–98 to 2000–01.

Since the NHL began adding new franchises in 1967, expansion had always led to an increase in offense. However, by 1996–97, goal scoring began to decline. That season, only Lemieux and Anaheim's Teemu Selanne managed to top 100 points (though Selanne's teammate Paul Kariya had 99). A year later, only Jagr reached triple digits and when he won the Art Ross Trophy again in 1999–2000, his 96 points were the fewest by a scoring leader since 1967–68. Part of the reason for the decline in scoring was tactical. Many coaches found it easier to keep their teams competitive if they emphasized defense. Part of the reason was also that bigger, faster and stronger players meant there was less open ice. But a big part of the reason was that the new generation of goaltenders was the most athletic and best-trained—not to mention best-protected—crop of netminders in NHL history.

Lighter materials for padding and better-designed masks allowed goalies to play lower to the ice than ever before. Patrick Roy perfected the

9

technique, bringing Glenn Hall's so-called "butterfly" style into the modern age. As Roy's wins—and Stanley Cup rings—piled up with the Montreal Canadiens and Colorado Avalanche, many younger goalies began to emulate him. Some, though, had a style all their own.

With a so-called "Slinky"—a child's toy spring which "walked" down stairs—for a spine, Dominik Hasek flipped and flopped his way to unprecedented success with the Buffalo Sabres. His 1.95 goals-against average in 1993–94 was the first below 2.00 since 1973–74 and gave him his first of six Vezina Trophy wins in an eight-year span. In 1996–97, New Jersey's Martin Brodeur led the NHL with a 1.88 goals-against average and 10 shutouts, making him the first goalie to reach double digits in shutouts since Ken Dryden in 1976–77. Still, not only the Vezina Trophy went to Hasek that year but also the Hart Trophy, making him just the fifth goalie to be named league MVP and the first since Jacques Plante in 1962. A year later, Hasek became the first goalie to win the Hart Trophy twice.

Fittingly, the 1990s ended with Wayne Gretzky's retirement in 1999 and his immediate election to the Hockey Hall of Fame.

Wayne Gretzky and the Sun Belt Kids

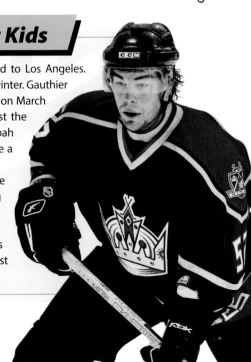

Gabe Gauthier was four years old when Wayne Gretzky was traded to Los Angeles. Gauthier's Canadian-born father put his California kid on skates that winter. Gauthier was hooked on hockey by the time he was eight. Fifteen years later, on March 11, 2007, he made his NHL debut with the Kings. Gauthier was just the second Southern California native to play for the team, joining Noah Clarke who, just one week later, became the first Californian to score a goal for Los Angeles.

In recent years, hockey programs like the Los Angeles Jr. Kings, the California Wave and the San Jose Jr. Sharks have started producing NHL prospects. The 2007 NHL Entry Draft also saw picks that had gotten their starts in other "non-traditional" hockey markets. Dallas native Austin Smith became the first Texan to be drafted by the Dallas Stars and the Columbus Blue Jackets made Trent Vogelhuber the first player ever drafted out of central Ohio.

The New Euro Invasion

The fall of Communism in the early 1990s allowed players from countries such as Russia and the former Czechoslovakia easy access to the NHL. This brand new pool of players helped the league expand, and led to full-scale NHL participation in hockey at the Winter Olympics.

1

Perestroika and Glasnost. The Fall of the Berlin Wall. The breakup of the Soviet Union. Events that changed the face of Europe also changed the face of the NHL during the 1990s, when scores of European players crossed the Atlantic to ply their trade in the expanding NHL.

"We can expand because of the Europeans," said former Anaheim coach Pierre Page of the NHL's growth from 21 to 30 teams in the 1990s. "We've gone from a redneck league to an international one." More and more U.S.-born players began to arrive as well, as the NHL of the 1990s evolved into a truly multinational entity.

In 1970, there was not one European player in the NHL. In 1990, there were 69. By 1997–98, the NHL had so many international players that the All-Star Game introduced a new format: North America versus The World.

In the Anaheim dressing room alone that year, six languages were spoken: English, French, Russian, Finnish, Swedish and Czech. "No other job you'd see that unless you were a U.N. ambassador," Ducks goalie Guy Hebert said. By the start of the 1999–2000 season, 28 percent of the NHL (183 players) was from Europe. There were 50 players in the NHL from the Czech Republic alone.

There were so many Czechs and Slovaks on the Pittsburgh Penguins in 1999–2000 that general manager Craig Patrick brought in Ivan Hlinka, who briefly played in the NHL and had coached the Czech Republic to Olympic gold in 1998, to work as an associate coach. (Hlinka and Finland's Alpo Suhonen in Chicago became the NHL's first European head coaches in 2000–01.) A quartet of Russians on the 2000 Cup-winning New Jersey Devils benefited greatly from the presence of assistant coach Slava Fetisov—a former star with the Soviet Red Army team who became one of the first Russian players to come to the NHL without having defected. The 1999–2000 Devils also featured the first U.S.-born Latino player in Scott Gomez.

During the 1970s, Borje Salming was the only European player honored at awards time as an NHL All-Star. Jari Kurri and four others were named throughout the 1980s. By 1997–98, Dominik Hasek, Nicklas Lidstrom, Peter Forsberg, and Jaromir Jagr, took four of the six positions on the First All-Star Team in a single season, and each was selected again the following year. Jagr led the NHL in

2

3

1: Helmet worn by Peter Forsberg as an NHL rookie in 1994–95.

2: The three Stastny brothers with the Quebec Nordiques in the 1980s.

3: Former Soviet star Viacheslav Fetisov entered the NHL with New Jersey Devils in 1989–90.

4: Russia-born Pittsburgh center Evgeni Malkin helped the Penguins return to the NHL summit.

5: Boston goalie Tuukka Rask ranked near the top for wins, save percentage and goals-against average.

6: Slovenian center Anze Kopitar joined the Los Angeles Kings in 2006–07.

4

5

The NHL at the Olympics

The 1998 Nagano Winter Games marked the first full-scale Olympic participation by NHL stars. The NHL's involvement resulted in the most evenly matched hockey competition in Olympic history—though North American fans were disappointed by the early elimination of the United States and by Canada's fourth-place finish. The Russians seemed headed for a gold medal until they ran into Dominik Hasek (arm rased, below) in the championship game. Hasek blanked Russia 1–0—Philadelphia Flyer Petr Svoboda scored in the third period—in the final to give the Czech Republic its first Olympic hockey gold.

The NHL continued in the Olympics at Salt Lake City in 2002, and this time Canada claimed its first hockey gold in 50 years with a victory over the U.S. in the final. Sweden won gold at Turin, Italy, in 2006 with a victory over their Finnish rivals. In 2010, Canada won gold on home ice in Vancouver, defeating the U.S. 3–2 on an overtime goal by Sidney Crosby. Canada won again at Sochi, Russia, in 2014, this time defeating Sweden 3–0 in the gold medal game.

Leadership issues may finally have been laid aside by Detroit's Stanley Cup success in the late 1990s and early 2000s with a lineup heavy on Swedes and Russians. By the start of the 2006–07 season, there were 13 European captains in the NHL.

These days, on NHL.com, "country" is just one of the many categories a user can select to break down statistics. In a quick alphabetical perusal there are players from Austria, Germany, Lithuania and Slovenia, as well as the more standard European hockey powers. Russians Alex Ovechkin and Evgeni Malkin are both multiple winners of the Art Ross Trophy as the NHL's top scorer, while Swedish twins, Daniel and Henrik Sedin, have each won it once. As for the Hart Trophy as MVP, Ovechkin (three times), Henrik Sedin, and Malkin have all won it. When seven-time Norris Trophy winner Nicklas Lidstrom played his final season in 2011–12, the trophy for best defenseman went to fellow Swede Erik Karlsson, while Henrik Lundqvist won the Vezina trophy as best goalie. But perhaps the best indication of the internationalization of the NHL is not the number of European stars but in the fact that so many teams use Canadians, Americans, and Europeans almost interchangeably as role players as well.

7

8

7: Detroit Red Wings jersey worn by four-time Stanley Cup winner Nicklas Lidstrom, a 20-year NHL veteran

8: Lidstrom was Detroit's alternate captain during the Red Wings' Stanley Cup wins of 1998 and 2002 and he was a gold medal-winner in the Winter Olympic Games (2006) and World Championship (1991) with Sweden.

scoring five times between 1994–95 and 2000–01, while Alex Mogilny, Teemu Selanne, Pavel Bure and Peter Bondra combined to lead the league in goals seven times in nine seasons from 1992–93 through 2000–01. Keith Tkachuk became the first American to lead the NHL in goals in 1996–97.

In 1993–94, Sergei Fedorov finished second to Wayne Gretzky in the scoring race, yet still became the first European player to win the Hart Trophy as league MVP. In an unprecedented display of all-around skill, Fedorov also won the Selke Trophy as the NHL's best defensive forward.

By the end of the 1990s, more Canadian kids than ever were going to U.S. colleges to prepare for NHL hockey, while European youngsters swarmed through the junior and minor professional leagues of North America. European-born players who could once be found only in the late rounds of the annual Entry Draft were now swelling the early rounds as well. Yet for all the advancements European players were making, there were still many who questioned their dedication and leadership, especially at playoff time. Though players such as Lars-Erik Sjoberg and Peter Stastny had served as captains in the 1970s and '80s, there were no European captains in the 1990s until the Toronto Maple Leafs stitched the 'C' on Mats Sundin's sweater before the 1997–98 season.

Chapter 5
The New Millennium

The first two decades of the 2000s featured the best of new and old in the National Hockey League. Wayne Gretzky passed the torch to a fresh crop of young stars—not only scorers, but also defensemen and spectacular goalies. New teams captured the Stanley Cup for the first time (including a couple in California). Meanwhile, a return to outdoor hockey became a smashing hit, and the NHL's 100th anniversary produced a parade of legends.

The NHL returned to its roots with the advent of hockey games outdoors.

Into The New Millennium

Milestones marked the beginning of the new millennium. So did defensive hockey. Patrick Roy set a new standard for career goalie wins, only to be surpassed by Martin Brodeur. And the Stanley Cup stopped by several places it had never been before, or hadn't visited in a long time.

Defense dominated as the NHL entered the 1999–2000 season, the first year of the post-Gretzky era. Among the goaltending fraternity, several new names emerged to join more familiar ones atop the statistics. Brian Boucher (1.91), Roman Turek (1.95) and Jose Theodore (2.10) finished 1–2–3 in goals-against average, though none of them would maintain that success. Among veteran goalies, Martin Brodeur led the league in wins (43) for the second straight season while Patrick Roy won 32 games to give him 444 victories in his career. Roy broke Terry Sawchuk's all-time record with his 448th regular-season victory on October 17, 2000, en route to a career-high 40 wins in 2000–01. Roy would climb to 551 wins by his retirement in 2003, but Brodeur would surpass his record total before the end of the first decade of the new millennium and soar well past 600 in the years beyond 2010.

The 2000–01 season was a year of milestones and accomplishments for many of the NHL's most respected veterans, capped off by a Stanley Cup victory for Raymond Bourque, the longtime Boston Bruins star who had joined the Colorado Avalanche at the trade deadline the year before. Bourque's first championship in the final season of his 22-year career was a fine finish to a campaign that had seen him surpass Paul Coffey as the top-scoring defenseman in NHL history. Teammate Joe Sakic also enjoyed an excellent year, joining Mark Messier, Wayne Gretzky and Bobby Clarke as only the fourth man to captain his team to a Stanley Cup title and win the Hart Trophy in the same year. Jaromir Jagr won his fourth straight scoring title, but the biggest story out of Pittsburgh came on December 27, 2000,

1: Long touted as a "can't miss" prospect, Sidney Crosby was a junior star at 16 in 2003–04 and 19 when the Pittsburgh Penguins named him team captain in 2007.

2: Injuries and illness kept Pittsburgh's Mario Lemieux—one of the NHL's very best— off the ice for long parts of the 1980s and '90s, but he made a remarkable comeback in 2000–01.

3: The first NHL Winter Classic was played in Buffalo on January 1, 2008, and 71,217 fans watched the Pittsburgh Penguins beat the Sabres.

4: The Chicago Blackhawks' young squad got better and better through the four rounds of the 2010 playoffs, and they won the Stanley Cup in six games against the Philadelphia Flyers.

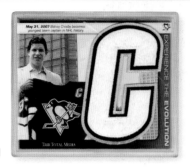

Young Stoppers in Goal

Though Martin Brodeur retired in 2015 with NHL career-leading totals of 691 wins and 125 shutouts, numbers which may be out of reach for all time, there are plenty of goalies in the league today that have established themselves in the elite class.

On March 9, 2014, Henrik Lundqvist won his 300th game, all with the New York Rangers. Nine days later, he won his 302nd game to surpass Mike Richter as the team's all-time leader. On March 22, 2014, Lundqvist blanked Brodeur and the New Jersey Devils 2–0 for his 50th career shutout, surpassing Ed Giacomin atop the Rangers' list.

Carey Price is still a long way from top spot in Montreal, but his gold medal performance for Team Canada in the 2014 Winter Olympic Games helped solidify his elite status. Marc-Andre Fleury helped Pittsburgh win the Stanley Cup in 2009, 2016 and 2017, and at his best he's among the cream, alongside Jonathan Quick (below), Tuukka Rask, Antti Niemi, and Corey Crawford.

when Mario Lemieux came down from the owner's box and returned to action as an active player. Lemieux set up a goal just 33 seconds into his first game back and finished the season with 35 goals and 41 assists in just 43 games. Sadly, injuries would again haunt Lemieux, though he was able to captain Team Canada to an Olympic gold medal in Salt Lake City in 2002.

Several new names joined the NHL's elite during the 2001–02 season. Calgary's Jarome Iginla won both the Maurice Richard Trophy with 52

5: Raymond Bourque said goodbye to the NHL in great style, winning the Stanley Cup with Colorado in 2001.

6: Canada took gold in the 2010 Vancouver Olympic

Games, thanks to Sidney Crosby's overtime goal.

7: With Olympic gold and a strong 2013–14 season, Montreal's Carey Price was one of the NHL's elite goaltenders.

goals and the Art Ross Trophy with 96 points, but was edged out for the Hart Trophy by Jose Theodore, who also finished ahead of Patrick Roy for the Vezina Trophy awarded to the League's top goaltender. In both cases, the balloting actually ended in a tie with Theodore declared the winner because he had received more first-place votes.

Defense remained dominant in 2002–03, especially in the playoffs. New Jersey's Martin Brodeur had his record-setting fourth 40-win season, topping the league for the fifth year in a row with 41. He also led with nine shutouts and won the Vezina Trophy for the first time in his career. In the Stanley Cup Final, Brodeur led the Devils past the Anaheim Ducks who rode the hot goaltending of Jean-Sebastien Giguere throughout the playoffs.

After a breakthrough season in 2002–03, the Tampa Bay Lightning won the Stanley Cup in 2003–04. Up-and-coming superstars Brad Richards, Vincent Lecavalier and Martin St. Louis led the Lightning. St. Louis had a league-best 94 points and won the Hart Trophy as MVP to go along with the Art Ross. New Jersey's Scott Niedermayer was another first-time trophy winner, taking the Norris Trophy as best defenseman while teammate Martin Brodeur received the Vezina Trophy for the second straight season.

The surprise leader in goals-against average in 2003–04 was Miikka Kiprusoff, whose mark of 1.69 was the NHL's lowest since 1939–40 (and Brian Elliott of St. Louis produced a microscopic 1.56 mark in 2011–12). Acquired by Calgary from San Jose early in the season, Kiprusoff not only sparked the Flames to their first playoff appearance since 1996, he led Calgary all the way to game seven of the Stanley Cup Final before finally falling one win short against the Lightning.

Tampa Bay's 2004 Cup win was five years after the Dallas Stars' victory and set the stage for even more southern exposure for the game's most famous trophy. The Carolina Hurricanes claimed the Cup in 2006, followed by the Anaheim Ducks 12 months later. Five years after that, in 2012, the Los Angeles Kings brought another championship to Southern California with their first Stanley Cup title since joining the NHL in 1967.

A year earlier, the Boston Bruins had ended a 39-year Stanley Cup drought with a game-seven victory over the Vancouver Canucks. Boston's victory came one year after the Blackhawks had ended an even longer wait. Chicago had waited since 1961 to celebrate with the Stanley Cup but, after a 49-year Cup hiatus, the Blackhawks won the Cup again in 2013 and 2016.

New Rules, New Stars

New rules introduced for 2005–06 opened up the game and Pittsburgh's Sidney Crosby and Alex Ovechkin of the Washington Capitals led a galaxy of exciting young stars. The NHL also targeted illegal checks and welcomed the return of a franchise in Winnipeg.

1

*T*hough the NHL lost the entire 2004–05 season to a difficult labor dispute, the League promised to be better than ever when action resumed in 2005–06. Not only was the new business model supposed to make it possible for every team to compete equally off the ice, the game on the ice would be improved too. The size of the offensive zones was increased, the center ice red line would no longer negate two-line "stretch" passes, restrictions were placed on the size of goaltenders' equipment, and shootouts were introduced to bring added excitement to the regular season by breaking ties that remained after overtime. Most importantly, the NHL promised it would crackdown on the obstruction fouls that had slowed the game in recent years.

The resulting increase in offense was impressive. Goal scoring jumped 18 percent over the previous season, going from 5.1 goals per game in 2003–04 to 6.1 goals per game in 2005–06. It was the biggest single-season jump since 1929–30 when forward passing was introduced to the offensive zone. Five players finished the season with 50 goals or more, and seven topped 100 points.

Because of the lockout, a "double cohort" of rookies entered the NHL in 2005–06. Both Alex Ovechkin (selected first overall in 2004) and Sidney Crosby (first in 2005) more than lived up to expectations. In Washington, Ovechkin became only the third rookie in NHL history to reach both 50 goals and 100 points. In Pittsburgh, Crosby became the youngest player in

NHL history to reach 100. The Ottawa Senators battled for the top spot in the Eastern Conference with the surprising Buffalo Sabres and Carolina Hurricanes, with the Hurricanes coming out on top in the playoffs. In the west, the Edmonton Oilers squeaked into the playoffs in eighth place before upsetting the top-ranked Red Wings, then San Jose and Anaheim en route to the Stanley Cup Final. The Cinderella run ended there, however, as Carolina defeated them in seven games.

The Senators reached the Stanley Cup Final for the first time in franchise history in 2006–07, but they were defeated by the Anaheim Ducks, who became the first Stanley Cup champions from California and the first West Coast team to win the trophy since the Victoria Cougars in 1925.

Just a couple of weeks after Carolina's Eric Staal led all playoff performers in scoring in 2006, his brother Jordan was selected second overall by the Penguins in the NHL Draft. Like his older brother, Jordan Staal jumped directly into the NHL as an 18-year-old, joining Sidney Crosby and fellow rookie Evgeni Malkin (whom Pittsburgh had picked second overall in 2004) in a Penguins lineup for 2006–07 that was filled

2

3

4

Montreal Canadiens Centennial

Winners of the Stanley Cup a record 24 times, professional hockey's oldest and most successful club celebrated its centennial in 2009. The 2008–09 season saw the Canadiens host the NHL All-Star Game and Entry Draft. Early in 2009–10, the club played a special centennial game, a 5–1 home win against the Boston Bruins on December 4, 2009, the 100th anniversary of its founding. Centennial celebrations began in 2005–06 when the first Dickie Moore, Yvan Cournoyer and Boom-Boom Geoffrion had their numbers retired. Seven other players would be so honored over the next four seasons. In addition, the Royal Canadian Mint and Canada Post issued commemorative coins and stamps, the club released a documentary, a book, a magazine, and a special set of collector cards. In addition, the Canadiens wore a variety of vintage jerseys from different eras, staged "Original Six" nights against their most storied opponents, and opened a Ring of Honor in the Bell Centre to celebrate Canadiens inducted into the Hockey Hall of Fame. Fittingly, it was the longest and grandest celebration ever staged by a hockey club anywhere in the world.

1: Detroit Red Wings championship ring, 2008.

Four young superstars to flourish in the 2010s NHL:
2: P.K. Subban, Montreal Canadiens defenseman.
3: Right wing for the Chicago Blackhawks, Patrick Kane.
4: Dallas Stars center Tyler Seguin.
5: Matt Duchene, Colorado Avalanche center.

6: The Chicago Blackhawks scored two goals in 17 seconds late in the third period to win the Stanley Cup in Game 6 of the 2013 Final.

7: Commemorative Stanley Cup medallion, Anaheim Ducks, 2007.

with so many talented youngsters it earned comparisons to the Edmonton Oilers of the 1980s. Malkin and Staal led another starry crop of NHL rookies that included Peter Stastny's son Paul with the Colorado Avalanche and Slovenian center Anze Kopitar with the Los Angeles Kings. Crosby became the first teenager in any major American sport to win a scoring title, leading the NHL with 120 points. The following season, the Penguins reached the Stanley Cup Final, losing to the Detroit Red Wings. A year later, both teams were back and this time it was Pittsburgh that came out on top, with Crosby becoming the youngest captain in history to lead his team to the Cup.

Patrick Kane, who had been selected first overall in 2007 and Jonathan Toews, chosen third in 2006, both joined the Chicago Blackhawks in 2007–08. Along with other young stars, such as defensemen Duncan Keith and Brent Seabrook, they quickly transformed an Original Six franchise that had fallen on hard times into one of the NHL's top teams, winning the Stanley Cup in 2010, 2013, and 2015. Talented young players continued to emerge. Defenseman Drew Doughty reminded many of the legendary Raymond Bourque when he entered the NHL in 2008–09 and has only gotten better, helping Los Angeles win the Stanley Cup in 2012 and and 2014, adding a second Olympic gold medal in 2014. Tampa Bay's Steven Stamkos was also a rookie in 2008–09. The first pick in the NHL Draft that year, Stamkos broke out in his sophomore season, scoring 51 goals in 2009–10 to tie Crosby for the League lead and added a League-leading 60 more in 2011–12. The 2011–12 season also saw the return of NHL hockey to Manitoba, where hockey-crazed citizens bought every available ticket and welcomed the former Atlanta Thrashers

as the newest incarnation of the Winnipeg Jets. Elsewhere that season, high draft pick —the second player chosen overall—Gabriel Landeskog made the team in Colorado as an 18-year-old rookie and joined Matt Duchene, who'd been the team's third pick in 2009. Landeskog was named the youngest captain in NHL history in 2012–13 and, in 2013–14, he and Duchene led the Avalanche back to the playoffs for the first time since 2010 under rookie head coach Patrick Roy who had his own track record of success in Colorado.

Despite a concussion that cost him parts of two seasons, Sidney Crosby has certainly proven that he belongs among the game's all-time greats, while Ovechkin, Kane, Toews and Stamkos are all firmly established as top stars. Only time will tell how many other talented newcomers to the NHL will add their names to the roll of legends that stretches from Joe Malone to Howie Morenz, Maurice Richard, Gordie Howe, Bobby Orr, Phil Esposito, Mike Bossy, Wayne Gretzky and Mario Lemieux.

8: 2006 Rookie of the Year Alex Ovechkin with the Calder Trophy.

9: 2007 NHL MVP Sidney Crosby with the Hart Trophy.

The NHL Outdoors

With the outdoor imagery harkening back to the roots of the game more than 100 years earlier, the National Hockey League has found great success with the NHL Heritage Classic, NHL Winter Classic, and NHL Stadium Series. Throw in the annual retro jerseys and it's a look that's hard to beat.

1

*T*he first time two NHL teams played a game outside it was anything but a NHL Winter Classic. Played on September 27, 1991, the preseason game between the New York Rangers and Los Angeles Kings took place in a parking lot outside the famous Caesars Palace Casino in Las Vegas. Temporary seats and a rink were set up, and a full house of 13,000 fans turned out. The temperature at the opening face-off was about 85° Fahrenheit (29°C) and went as high as 95°F (35°C) during the course of the game. Wayne Gretzky led the Kings to a 5–2 win over the Rangers. "We kept looking at each other," Gretzky remembered, "and we couldn't believe we were playing hockey in 80-degree weather. But it was real nice."

It was considerably colder the next time the NHL ventured outdoors.

The Edmonton Oilers had suggested the idea of hosting a Russian team in an outdoor game in the mid 1980s, but were turned down by then NHL President John Ziegler. It wasn't until 74,544 fans packed Spartan Stadium to see longtime rivals Michigan State University and the University of Michigan face-off on October 6, 2001, in a game dubbed the "Cold War," that the NHL embraced the concept. On November 22, 2003, a crowd of 57,167 filled Commonwealth Stadium in Edmonton (home of the Eskimos of the Canadian Football League) despite freezing temperatures of –18°Celsius (0°F), for the NHL Heritage Classic. Though he was still active with the New York Rangers, Mark Messier was given permission to suit up for the Oilers' alumni and he and Wayne Gretzky led the stars of Edmonton's 1980s dynasty to a 2–0 victory over the stars of Montreal's 1970s dynasty in an "MegaStars" exhibition before the main event. The Canadiens won that game 4–3 and the enduring image of the evening was goalie Jose Theodore wearing a Canadiens toque atop his mask.

Building on the success of the NHL Heritage Classic, in 2004 NBC pitched the NHL on the idea of the NHL Winter Classic. It took some time

1: Program from the Los Angeles Kings vs. Anaheim Ducks game at Dodger Stadium, January 25, 2014.

2: In 2014, the Anaheim Ducks beat the Los Angeles Kings 3–0 in an outdoor night game in front of 54,099 at Dodger Stadium.

3: Ryan Miller makes a save at the first NHL Winter Classic. The game, in Buffalo on January 1, 2008, attracted more than 70,000 fans.

2

3

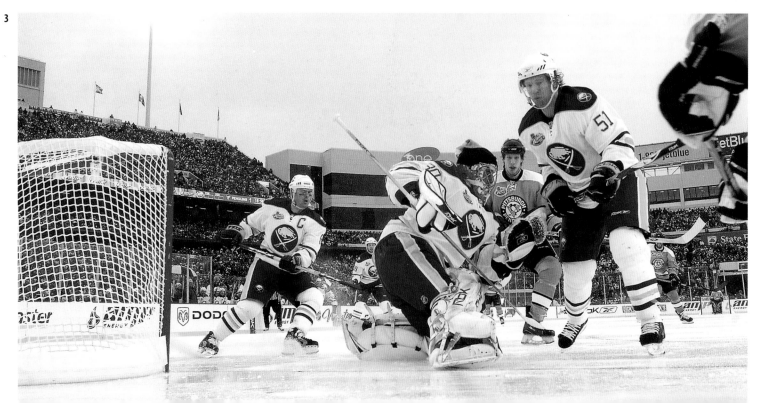

European vacation

The first time NHL teams played outside of North America was in 1938, when the Montreal Canadiens and Detroit Red Wings played a nine-game postseason series in England and France. Over the years, a handful of other teams made similar trips either before or after the NHL season.

The first time the NHL scheduled regular-season games overseas was in October of 1997 when Vancouver and Anaheim opened the schedule in Tokyo prior to the Nagano Olympics. There were further trips to Japan in 1998 and 2000. Then, between 2007 and 2011, the NHL opened the season with a series of games in several European cities. Fans in London, Prague, Stockholm, Helsinki and Berlin were treated to games involving several NHL teams.

While preparing to open the season in Europe in 2008 and 2009, the New York Rangers and Chicago Blackhawks took part in a competition with European teams for the Victoria Cup. The Rangers defeated Metallurg Magnitogorsk in 2008, while Chicago lost to ZCS Lions Zurich in 2009.

to make it all come together, but on January 1, 2008, the Buffalo Sabres hosted the Pittsburgh Penguins at Ralph Wilson Stadium, home of the NFL's Buffalo Bills. The game drew a crowd of 71,217, and they watched Sidney Crosby score the winning goal in a shootout during a light snowfall to give the Penguins a 2–1 victory. Television ratings were such a success that a New Year's tradition was born. On January 1, 2009, a crowd of 40,818

filled iconic Wrigley Field in Chicago to see the visiting Detroit Red Wings beat the hometown Blackhawks. In 2010, there were 38,112 in attendance at Boston's Fenway Park to see the Bruins beat the Philadelphia Flyers 2–1.

Though CBC had been enjoying large rating in Canada along with NBC in the United States, more Canadian teams wanted in on the outdoor action. So in addition to the NHL Winter Classic in Pittsburgh in 2011 (which drew 68,111 fans), a second NHL Heritage Classic was held on February 20, 2011. This one saw the Calgary Flames beat the Montreal Canadiens 4–0 in front of 41,022 fans.

After another successful NHL Winter Classic drew 46,967 fans to Citizens Bank Park in Philadelphia in 2012, the NHL proposed six outdoor games for 2014, adding a four-game NHL Stadium Series to the NHL Winter Classic and NHL Heritage Classic. For those who worried this would be too much of a good thing, NHL Commissioner Gary Bettman pointed out it was simply a case of supply and demand. "For teams and markets that want to host this [event], for fans that want to attend, we can't do enough of them," he explained.

Despite cold temperatures and snow that fell throughout the game, a record attendance of 105,491 at Michigan Stadium in Ann Arbor saw the Toronto Maple Leafs defeat the Detroit Red Wings 3–2 in a shootout on New Year's Day. The CBC drew record ratings in Canada for a non-playoff game and NBC had a huge American audience as well. Cold was certainly not a problem at Dodger Stadium, Los Angeles, when the Kings hosted the Anaheim Ducks on a beautiful night for the highly anticipated opener of the NHL Stadium Series on January 25, 2014. A crowd of 54,099 saw the Ducks record a 4–0 victory. The following afternoon, there were 50,105 on hand as the New York Rangers defeated the New Jersey Devils 7–3 at Yankee Stadium. The Rangers went on to complete a doubleheader sweep by beating the New York Islanders 2–1 on January 29. The NHL Stadium Series wrapped up with the Chicago Blackhawks beating the Pittsburgh Penguins 5–1 in front of 62,921 fans at Soldier Field on March 1, while a crowd of 54,194 saw the Ottawa Senators beat the Vancouver Canucks 4–2 the next night in the 2014 NHL Heritage Classic. It was the first stadium-based game to be played indoors—under the retractable roof of B.C. Place Stadium.

4: The Boston Bruins and Phoenix Coyotes played two games in Prague, Czech Republic, at the start of the 2010–11 season.

5: Special logo produced for the Prague games.

6: The largest crowd to ever witness a hockey game, 105,491, saw the Toronto Maple Leafs defeat the Detroit Red Wings 3-2 in a shootout on January 1, 2014.

7: The New York Rangers won back-to-back outdoor games at Yankee Stadium against local rivals the New Jersey Devils and New York Islanders on January 26 and 29, 2014.

The Stanley Cup had been contested for almost a quarter of a century before the birth of the National Hockey League in 1917. There will be more than a year of celebrations to mark the Centennial of the NHL, running through the calendar year of 2017 and the 2017–18 hockey season.

When the clock struck midnight on December 31, 2016, five of the greatest players from the early days of the NHL were gathered at a hotel in Toronto. Red Kelly, at 89 years old the elder statesman of the group, along with goaltender Glenn Hall, and forwards John Bucyk, Alex Delvecchio, and Dave Keon, were about to drop the puck on a year-long hockey celebration.

None of them were born when the NHL officially began in 1917, but they were voted by a panel of experts to be among the 100 greatest players in NHL history. The day after their New Year's Eve gathering, these five men were introduced in a ceremony prior to the start of the NHL Centennial Classic, an outdoor game between the Red Wings and Maple Leafs at Toronto's Exhibition Stadium. This would be the beginning of a yearlong celebration of the NHL's 100th anniversary.

The first official NHL game was played on December 19, 1917 between the Montreal Wanderers and the Toronto Arenas. Only 700 fans were in attendance for the game (even though World War I soldiers in uniform were invited for free). As just one small sign of how far the NHL has come since then, more than 40,000 fans filled Exhibition Stadium to see the NHL Centennial Classic game.

The rollout of the "100 Greatest NHL Players" was the centerpiece of the centennial celebration. The ceremony at the Centennial Classic unveiled the first 33 players on the list, representing the league's first 50 years. Less than a month later, at the NHL All-Star Game weekend in Los Angeles, the remaining 67 players, representing the modern era of pro hockey, were

1: The NHL produced special Centennial logos to celebrate the League's 100 years and incorporating the Stanley Cup.

2: Bobby Orr, 4 (faced by Drew Doughty, 8), and Mark Messier, 11 (Jeff Carter, 77), were among the legends on hand for the ceremonial puck drop before the 2017 NHL All-Star Game at Staples Center in Los Angeles.

3: The NHL Centennial Classic, on January 1, 2017, featured the Toronto Maple Leafs— successors to the original Toronto Arenas—and "Original Six" team Detroit Red Wings, the game being played at Exhibition Stadium in Toronto.

4: A gala evening celebrated the announcement of the 100 Greatest NHL Players

5: The NHL had a float at the annual Pasadena Tournament of Roses Parade on New Year's Day 2017.

6: Left to right, Ron McLean, Glenn Hall, Johnny Bucyk, Red Kelly, Johnny Bower, Dave Keon and Wayne Gretzy are feted by fans at Exhibition Stadium, Toronto, before the NHL Centennial Classic game.

5

4

announced during "The NHL 100," a gala event at Microsoft Theater on January 27.

Of the 67 legends announced, 48 were on hand at the event, making for an awe-inspiring moment when they all took the stage together.

"It's humbling to be here today," Mark Messier told NHL.com's Dave Stubbs during a private reception before the gala. "I probably played against most of these guys. If not, then I watched them intently growing up. And if they're older than that, then I knew about them through the history of the game. I'm not sure if there's been an event I've been to since being a part of the NHL that has had a room full of so many incredible ambassadors of this magnitude."

In addition to being honored at live events throughout 2017, the NHL's 100 greatest were immortalized on canvas. The league commissioned Canadian artist Tony Harris to paint original portraits of each player. The 11-by-14 oil-based portraits were digitized and NHL.com unveiled two each week of the year.

Fans across North America were able to join the anniversary festivities by visiting the NHL Centennial Fan Arena—a traveling museum of sorts that made stops at various league venues throughout 2017. The exhibit consisted of a 53-foot truck with custom interior featuring more than 1,000 square feet of interactive digital displays, original video content, historical memorabilia and unique photos. A second trailer hosted a giant video screen. A pop-up was on hand for youth games and clinics, while a virtual reality experience allowed fans to ride a Zamboni as if they were on the ice.

As a philanthropic component to the centennial celebration, the NHL donated $5,000 to every NHL team to contribute to their respective communities. The grants were to be used to promote inclusiveness and diversity in hockey.

Coincidentally, 2017 also marked the 125th anniversary of the Stanley Cup. This occasion was celebrated in March, when the trophy went on display at Rideau Hall in Ottawa, Canada. Rideau Hall, the residence of the Governor General of Canada, is where Lord Stanley of Preston was residing when he came up with the idea of the Stanley Cup in 1892.

As part of the celebration, fans were able to have their picture taken with the Cup, under the official portrait of Lord Stanley.

Both the Stanley Cup and NHL anniversary events provided a rush for all hockey fans. Even NHL commissioner Gary Bettman got caught up in the magnitude, talking at that private dinner on December 31, 2016, about how he felt when he called players to inform them they were voted to the centennial celebration team.

"I was more excited about those calls than anybody who I called," said Bettman. "It was such an honor, it was such a thrill … Up until that point, whenever I was asked, 'What's the best thing about being commissioner of the NHL?' I would say, 'Presenting the Stanley Cup.' I've gotta tell you, this once-in-a-100-year thing is very, very special."

The NHL 100

The centerpiece of the National Hockey League's centennial celebration was the unveiling of the 100 greatest players in league history. The players—chosen by a Blue Ribbon panel comprised of former players, league executives and respected media members—included 33 players from the NHL's first 50 years and another 67 from the modern day era.

Here are the "NHL 100:"

Sid Abel	Wayne Gretzky	Bobby Orr
Syl Apps	Glenn Hall	Alex Ovechkin
Andy Bathgate	Doug Harvey	Bernie Parent
Jean Beliveau	Dominik Hasek	Brad Park
Max Bentley	Tim Horton	Gilbert Perreault
Toe Blake	Gordie Howe	Jacques Plante
Mike Bossy	Bobby Hull	Denis Potvin
Ray Bourque	Brett Hull	Chris Pronger
Johnny Bower	Jaromir Jagr	Jean Ratelle
Turk Broda	Patrick Kane	Henri Richard
Martin Brodeur	Duncan Keith	Maurice Richard
Johnny Bucyk	Red Kelly	Larry Robinson
Pavel Bure	Ted Kennedy	Luc Robitaille
Chris Chelios	Dave Keon	Patrick Roy
King Clancy	Jari Kurri	Joe Sakic
Bobby Clarke	Elmer Lach	Borje Salming
Paul Coffey	Guy Lafleur	Denis Savard
Charlie Conacher	Pat LaFontaine	Serge Savard
Yvan Cournoyer	Brian Leetch	Terry Sawchuk
Sidney Crosby	Jacques Lemaire	Milt Schmidt
Pavel Datsyuk	Mario Lemieux	Teemu Selanne
Alex Delvecchio	Nicklas Lidstrom	Brendan Shanahan
Marcel Dionne	Eric Lindros	Eddie Shore
Ken Dryden	Ted Lindsay	Darryl Sittler
Bill Durnan	Al MacInnis	Billy Smith
Phil Esposito	Frank Mahovlich	Peter Stastny
Tony Esposito	Mark Messier	Scott Stevens
Sergei Fedorov	Stan Mikita	Mats Sundin
Peter Forsberg	Mike Modano	Jonathan Toews
Ron Francis	Dickie Moore	Bryan Trottier
Grant Fuhr	Howie Morenz	Georges Vezina
Bob Gainey	Scott Niedermayer	Steve Yzerman
Mike Gartner	Joe Nieuwendyk	
Bernie Geoffrion	Adam Oates	

6:

Chapter 6
Legends of Hockey

Learn more about the colorful names and fierce rivalries that have contributed to the rich history of the National Hockey League. Players such as Georges Vezina, Frank Boucher, and Doug Harvey paved the way for the likes of Martin Brodeur, Gordie Howe, and Bobby Orr. Coaches used to be former star players but that is a rarity these days. One of the most decorated coaches in NHL history, in fact, was a policeman by trade.

The New York Americans was the first team to play at Madison Square Garden.

Great Goaltenders

Throughout hockey history, the greatest goaltenders have played their best under pressure. The finest goalies combine focus and quick reflexes with the ability to bounce back quickly from their mistakes as well as great bravery and instinctive reactions.

1

Georges Vezina helped the Montreal Canadiens win either the NHA or the NHL title on five occasions, and the Stanley Cup in 1916 and 1924. His career began when the rules required him to remain on his feet, so his early numbers are less impressive than those who came later, but he led the NHL in goals-against average in its first season of 1917–18.

Vezina had joined the Canadiens in 1910–11 and never missed a game, regular-season or playoffs, for the next 15 years. His 367-game streak ended on November 28, 1925, when chest pains forced him out of action. He never played again, and died of tuberculosis on March 26, 1926. Canadiens ownership donated the Vezina Trophy to honor his memory, yet even in his prime, it would be hard to argue that Vezina was a better goalie than Clint Benedict. Benedict joined the Ottawa Senators in 1912–13. He won the Stanley Cup with Ottawa in 1920, 1921, and 1923, and with the Montreal Maroons in 1926. He also led the NHL in goals-against average every season from 1918–19 through 1922–23, and in 1926–27. More importantly, his habit of "accidentally" falling to the ice to stop shots and cover loose pucks forced

the NHL to adopt the PCHA rule that allowed goalies to leave their feet. On February 20, 1930, Benedict became the first NHL goalie to wear a mask in a game.

Good as Vezina and Benedict were, they had nothing on the generation of goaltenders that followed them. In 1928–29, when George Hainsworth registered 22 shutouts and 0.92 goals-against average, eight of the NHL's top 10 goaltenders had at least 10 shutouts and all 10 had averages below 2.00. Netminders like Boston's Tiny Thompson, Chicago's Chuck Gardiner, and Roy Worters of the New York Americans ranked among the best in the NHL for years. Hainsworth won the Vezina Trophy in 1928–29, but Worters, who posted a 1.15 goals-against average and 13 shutouts to lead the Americans into the playoffs after a last-place finish the year before, became the first goaltender to win the Hart Trophy as the NHL's most valuable player. Since then, only goalies Chuck Rayner (1949–50), Al Rollins (1953–54), Jacques Plante (1961–62) Dominik Hasek (1996–97 and 1997–98) and Jose Theodore (2001–02) have been named NHL MVP.

The Toronto Maple Leafs' Frank McCool turned in one of the most amazing performances by a rookie netminder in 1944–45. But McCool, who was known as "Ulcers," doubled up in pain regularly during the 1945 playoffs, even after posting three straight shutouts against Detroit in the Stanley Cup Final. He played only part of one more NHL season before retiring from hockey.

Bill Durnan was another great goalie that battled the pressure. Durnan played seven seasons for the Montreal Canadiens beginning in 1943–44

1: Clint Benedict sports the NHL's first goalie mask.

2: Glenn Hall of the Chicago Blackhawks.

3: Georges Vezina of Montreal.

4: Terry Sawchuck posted great numbers with the Detroit Red Wings in the 1950s.

5: George Hainsworth (left) and Roy Worters, two big stars of the late 1920s and 1930s.

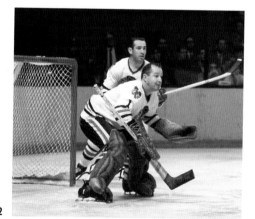
2

4

5

Jacques Plante and the Goalie Mask

6: Belly pad worn by Cesare Maniago in the 1960s and '70s.

7: Blocker and catcher worn by Terry Sawchuk.

8: Martin Brodeur of the New Jersey Devils.

9: Patrick Roy was the first goalie in NHL history to record 500 career wins. He retired with 551 regular-season victories plus 151 more in the playoffs.

Jacques Plante, who won the Vezina Trophy a record seven times, was perhaps the most influential goalie in hockey history. His roaming style changed the way the position was played, and he popularized the mask after wearing one in an NHL game on November 1, 1959.

But neither Jacques Plante nor Clint Benedict was the first goalie to wear a mask. In December of 1903, Eddie Giroux of the Toronto Marlboros donned a baseball catcher's mask in practice after taking a puck in the face. In December of 1921 it was proposed to allow goalies to wear catcher's masks in the Ontario Hockey Association, but Elizabeth Graham of the Queen's University women's team is thought to be the first goalie to wear a mask (a fencing mask) in a game in 1927. After Clint Benedict was hurt in 1930, the *Montreal Gazette* speculated that, "some day, the league will authorize masks for netminders as baseball does for its catchers...." Gerry Cheevers went a step further by decorating his protection with "stitches" showing the possible injuries to his face the mask had helped to avoid.

and won the Vezina Trophy six times, but the stress of the game's most difficult position caused his retirement in 1950.

Perhaps there has never been a better collection of goaltending talent together in the NHL as there was in the 1950s and '60s. But men like Terry Sawchuk, Johnny Bower, Glenn Hall, Gump Worsley and Jacques Plante battled demons too. "How would you like it," Plante once said, "if you were out on your job or in your office and you made a little mistake. Suddenly a bright red light flashed on behind you and then 18,000 people started screaming...?" Sawchuk may have looked as if he would rather not have been on the ice, but he posted 447 victories in his 21-year career, and 103 shutouts.

Better equipment—and a better understanding of the psychology and technique—has changed how goaltenders go about their jobs. Terry Sawchuk played in a deep crouch that paved the way for Glenn Hall's butterfly style, but it wasn't until newer, lighter equipment made goaltending safer that Patrick Roy could truly perfect the butterfly.

A new generation of goalies could now play low along the ice, taking away the bottom of the net. Roy was the first goalie to surpass Sawchuk's win total, only to be surpassed himself by Martin Brodeur, who retired with 691 regular season wins, plus another 113 in playoffs. Brodeur remains the only goalie to break Sawchuk's shutout record, but Ed Belfour, Curtis Joseph, and Roberto Luongo—who passed him in 2016–17—also bettered his 447 wins.

Today, there are great goaltenders in the NHL from all around the world. Sweden's Henrik Lundqvist has topped 30 wins in every complete season he's played since entering the NHL in 2005–06 and surpassed Mike Richter as the winningest goalie in New York Rangers history in 2013–14. Lundqvist, Sergei Bobrovsky (Russia), Tim Thomas (USA), Ryan Miller (USA) and the now retired Miikka Kiprusoff (Finland) are all recent winners of the Vezina Trophy. Thomas and Jonathan Quick, another American, are both recent winners of the Conn Smythe Trophy as playoff MVP for leading Boston (2011) and Los Angeles (2012) to the Stanley Cup. Though he was never able to win the Stanley Cup with the Vancouver Canucks, Roberto Luongo does have two Olympic Games gold medals with Team Canada and ended the 2016–17 season leading the way with most wins by an active NHL goaltender, with 453.

Colorful combinations such as the "Kraut Line," the "Punch Line," the "Production Line," and the "French Connection," were as familiar to fans as the names of their favorite players and favorite teams. In the NHL of the 21st century, it seems that set forward lines have gone the way of the rover and the leather helmet.

Constant line juggling by coaches today means that few players get to line up together for an extended period. There are many fans around the NHL who miss the glamor and excitement of these attacking combos.

In the NHL's early days, offense was based mainly on individual talent. In a time before forward passing, speed and stickhandling were a player's greatest assets. "Combination play" was always considered important, but the new emphasis on offense in the 1930s and '40s finally placed a premium on cohesive team play. Forward lines came to the fore, and the best were often given inspiring nicknames that helped capture fans imaginations.

The first of the NHL's great lines was the New York Rangers trio of Bill Cook, Frank Boucher, and Bun Cook. Though sometimes referred to as the A Line (for the Subway Line that ran below the old Madison Square Garden), or, erroneously, as the Bread Line (which was actually a later Rangers' combo of Alex Shibicky with brothers Mac and Neil Colville), the trio was usually known simply as the Boucher–Cook line. Teamed up for the Rangers' first season of 1926–27, the elegant Boucher became the game's best passer and winner of the Lady Byng Trophy seven times in eight years between 1927–28 and 1934–35. Bill Cook was one of the NHL's most dangerous scorers, and together with his brother Bun, they devised passing patterns that revolutionized offensive play and helped the Rangers win the Stanley Cup in 1928 and 1933.

In Boston, the "Dynamite Line" of Cooney Weiland, Dit Clapper and Dutch Gainor helped the Bruins follow up their first Stanley Cup victory in 1928–29 with a record of 38–5–1 in 1929–30 for an .875 winning percentage that remains the best in NHL history. Weiland led the NHL with 43 goals and 73 points in 44 games in 1929–30, but the Hart Trophy for the league's most valuable player went to Nels Stewart of the Montreal Maroons. Stewart was triggerman for the powerful "S-Line," with Babe Seibert and Hooley Smith. The rival Canadiens were led by Howie Morenz, who, as the fastest player of his generation, had been more than able to hold his own as an individual icon. He and Aurel Joliat had become a very dangerous duo, and teamed with Johnny

1: "Kraut Line" center Milt Schmidt of the Boston Bruins.

2: Chicago Black Hawks puck.

3: New York Rangers linemates Rod Gilbert, Vic Hadfield and Jean Ratelle celebrate a goal.

4: Toronto's "Kid Line" of Charlie Conacher, Joe Primeau and Busher Jackson.

5: The three NHL Bentley brothers: Reg, Max and Doug. Max and Doug starred with Bill Mosienko on Chicago's "Pony Line."

The 1960s had its share of interesting line combinations, most notably in Chicago where the Blackhawks had the "Million Dollar Line" of Bobby Hull, Bill Hay and Murray Balfour and the "Scooter Line" of Doug Mohns, Stan Mikita and Kenny Wharram. In the 1970s, the New York Rangers had the "G-A-G Line" of Vic Hadfield, Jean Ratelle and Rod Gilbert—so named for their "Goal-A-Game" production. For sheer numbers, the Boston Bruins' line of Phil Esposito, Ken Hodge and Wayne Cashman was one of the NHL's most prolific ever, but they had no catchy nickname. Sometimes known as the Dogs of War, they were usually just called the Espo line.

The best name of the 1970s belongs to Buffalo Sabres linemates Richard Martin, Gilbert Perreault, and Rene Robert, who were dubbed the "French Connection." The name reflects both the Quebec birthplace of the three players and the 1971 hit movie of the same name.

6: New York Rangers stars Bill Cook, Frank Boucher and Bun Cook.

7: Gordie Howe, Sid Abel and Ted Lindsay of Detroit's famed and feared "Production Line."

8: Boston Bruins jersey worn by Dit Clapper, a member of the record-setting "Dynamite Line."

9: Richard Martin starred on the Buffalo Sabres' "French Connection" line in the 1970s.

Gagnon in 1930–31, they became a terrific trio known as the "Speedball Line."

In Toronto, the Maple Leafs put youngsters Busher Jackson, Joe Primeau, and Charlie Conacher together in 1929–30. Dubbed the "Kid Line," they were prolific scorers and finished first, second, and fourth in the NHL scoring race in 1931–32 and led the Maple Leafs to the Stanley Cup. Later in the decade, the Bruins unveiled the "Kraut Line" of Milt Schmidt, Bobby Bauer and Woody Dumart (all three hailed from the German-heritage area of Kitchener, Ontario), who led Boston to Stanley Cup titles in 1938–39 and 1940–41.

Maurice Richard's rookie season was cut short by injuries in 1942–43, but in 1943–44, Canadiens coach Dick Irvin teamed him with Toe Blake and Elmer Lach and the "Punch Line" was born. The talented trio practically re-wrote the NHL record book while leading Montreal to Stanley Cup titles in 1944 and 1946. The 1945–46 season saw brothers Max and Doug Bentley teamed with Bill Mosienko on the "Pony Line" in Chicago. Though the Blackhawks struggled, this line was among the best in the NHL, with Max Bentley winning the scoring title two years in a row.

Gordie Howe was first teamed with Sid Abel and Ted Lindsay in Detroit 1946–47. In 1948–49 they were dubbed the "Production Line" for their offensive prowess and the production of the assembly lines in the car plants of the Motor City. Lindsay and Howe (twice) won scoring titles in three of the four seasons the line spent together, and Detroit won the Stanley Cup in 1950 and 1952. Later in the 1950s, the Bruins had the "Uke Line" of Johnny Bucyk, Bronco Horvath and Vic Stasiuk, who were all of Ukrainian heritage.

Triple Crown and the Trio Grande

During the 1980–81 season, the Los Angeles Kings' "Triple Crown" line of Dave Taylor, Marcel Dionne and Charlie Simmer became the first line in NHL history where all three players topped 100 points. Both Simmer and Dionne had also topped 100 the year before, when Dionne won the Art Ross Trophy as the league's top scorer. Before teaming up with Dionne in 1978–79, Simmer had been a career minor leaguer and Taylor was a virtually unknown second-year player.

While Dionne, Simmer and Taylor were lighting up scoreboards on the west coast, the New York Islanders' combination of Clark Gillies, Bryan Trottier and Mike Bossy was doing the same in the east. Two years before the Triple Crown players each reached 100, Bryan Trottier led the NHL with 134 points, while Mike Bossy had 126 and Gillies had 91. This threesome was known as the "Trio Grande," though they were sometimes called the "Long Island Electric Company."

Family Dynasties

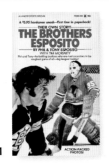

Hockey has seen more than its share of famous families As hockey talent often seems to be in the genes. Family dynasties have sprung up from all over, be it in Viking, Alberta, or Warroad, Minnesota, or Ornskoldsvik, Sweden. Every era, it seems, brings out another group, be they brothers, cousins or from different generations.

More than 100 father and son combinations, as well as over 200 brothers, have appeared in the NHL over the years. There are even families that can boast three generations of hockey stars. Brothers Lester and Frank Patrick both dominated as players in several leagues from 1904 until the mid-1920s before becoming coaches and managers in the NHL. Lester's sons, Lynn and Muzz, both followed in their father's footsteps. They played together under their famous father with the New York Rangers and both also went on to successful careers in hockey management. Lynn's boys, Glenn and Craig, also made the NHL as players, with Craig going on to win the Stanley Cup twice as the general manager of the Pittsburgh Penguins. Lester, Frank, Lynn and Craig are all Honoured Members of the Hockey Hall of Fame.

Another three-generation family is the Hextalls. Hall of Famer Bryan Hextall played with Lynn and Muzz Patrick on the Rangers of the 1930s and 1940s. Sons Bryan Jr. and Dennis played with several teams in the 1960s and '70s, while Bryan Jr.'s son Ron was a goalie in the NHL in the 1980s and '90s. On December 8, 1987, Ron Hextall became the first goalie in league history to shoot a puck the length of the ice for a goal.

Bernie "Boom Boom" Geoffrion is a future Hall of Famer who starred with the Montreal Canadiens in the 1950s. His son Danny spent 32 games with the Canadiens during his brief NHL career in the 1980s. Danny's son Blake seemed destined for better things. Drafted by Nashville but later traded to Montreal, Blake Geoffrion's career was cut short by a fractured skull suffered while playing in the minors in 2012. Blake was not just a third generation Geoffrion, but also the NHL's first fourth generation player. "Boom Boom"

had been married to the daughter of legendary Canadiens star Howie Morenz, which makes Morenz Blake's great-grandfather.

Talent is not always evenly distributed among hockey families. Brothers Charlie, Roy, and Lionel Conacher each played their way into the Hockey Hall of Fame during the 1930s and '40s, but Charlie's son Pete and Lionel's son Brian were far less successful. Max and Doug Bentley also made the Hall of Fame, but older brother Reg Bentley lasted only 11 games in the NHL. Charlie and Roy Conacher and Max and Doug Bentley were all NHL scoring champions, a sibling feat unmatched until twin brothers Henrik and Daniel Sedin won back-to-back scoring titles with the Vancouver Canucks in 2009–10 and 2010–11.

People still argue about whether Gordie Howe or Maurice Richard was the best player of his generation, but there's no argument as to who had the better brother. Maurice and Henri

1: The book The Brothers Esposito came out in 1971. Phil and Tony were both NHL superstars.

2: Blackhawks Dwayne (left) and Brent Sutter are two of the nine family members to have played in the NHL.

3: Brothers and teammates Lynn and Muzz Patrick flank their father, Rangers GM Lester Patrick.

4: Flyers goalie Ron Hextall was a rare third generation NHL star.

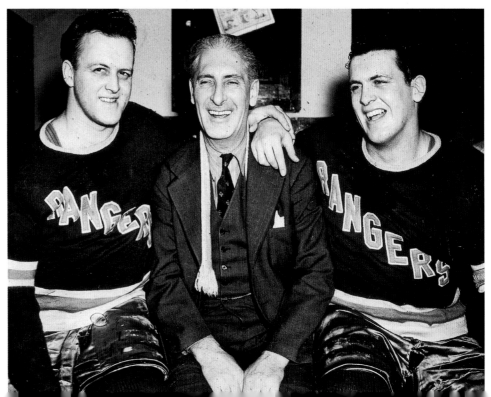

Richard combined to score 902 goals in their storied careers. The Howe brothers notched 804 goals, but Vic Howe only had three of them during the 33 games he played over parts of three seasons with the New York Rangers. Wayne Gretzky and his brother Brent scored 895 goals, but their totals are even more lopsided than the Howes with Wayne leading 894–1. Phil Esposito outscored his brother Tony 717–0 … but, of course, Tony was one of the top goalies in NHL history. When Ken Dryden of the Montreal Canadiens faced his older brother Dave with the Buffalo Sabres on March 20, 1971, it marked the only time in NHL history that two brothers opposed each other as goalies in the same game.

When it comes to fathers and sons, both the Howes and the Hulls have made their mark. Bobby's son Brett managed to outscore his famous father (and everybody else in hockey history except Gordie Howe, Wayne Gretzky and Jaromir Jagr) with 741 goals. Gordie's sons couldn't beat him, but they did join him! Gordie, Mark and Marty Howe spent six years as teammates

5

The Christians

Gordon Christian represented the United States at the 1955 World Championships and won a silver medal at the 1956 Winter Olympics. His brothers Bill and Roger joined him on the U.S. national team in 1957–58 and were stars on the 1960 team that won a surprising gold medal at the Squaw Valley Olympics. (Brothers Bill and Bob Cleary also starred on the 1960 U.S. team.) Twenty years later, Bill Christian's son Dave won gold with the "Miracle on Ice" team at the Lake Placid Olympics before embarking on a 15-year NHL career.

The Christian brothers' father was a carpenter, and Roger and Bill worked with him in the offseason. In 1964, they began their own hockey stick company. By the mid 1980s, Christian Brothers Hockey (which also made pants and gloves) was churning out a half-million sticks per year from their factory in Warroad, Minnesota. The company lives on today in partnership with Harrow Sports.

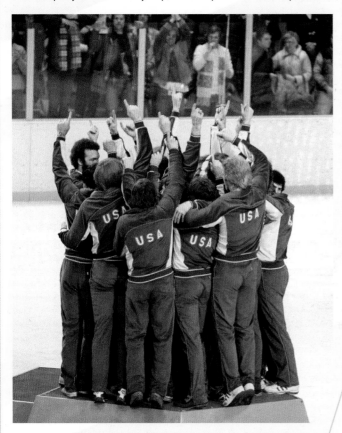

6

5: Jordan (#12) and Eric Staal are two of four brothers from Thunder Bay, Ontario, to play in the NHL.

6: Dave Dryden of the Buffalo Sabres with his kid brother Ken of the Montreal Canadiens.

in the World Hockey Association, and one together in the NHL with the Hartford Whalers. Mark went on to become an NHL star in his own right.

Born while their father was starring in Detroit, both Mark and Marty Howe were Americans. So were the Broten brothers of Roseau, Minnesota. Aaron and Paul Broten had their moments, but Neal was the most successful. An Olympic gold medalist as part of the "Miracle on Ice" team at Lake Placid in 1980, Neal went on to play 1,099 NHL games over 17 seasons. His 923 points (289 goals, 634 assists) were the most by an American until being surpassed by Joe Mullen, who was himself part of a pretty fine family tandem with his brother Brian.

When it comes to sheer numbers, no family is likely to match the Sutters of Viking, Alberta. Six Sutters—Brian, Brent, Darryl, Dwayne, Rich and Ron—were all active in the NHL at the same time between 1982–83 and 1986–87. To date, Brent's son Brandon, Darryl's son Brett, Dwayne's son Brody have brought the family's NHL total to nine, while Rich's son Lukas and Ron's son Riley toil hopefully in the minors.

Four Staal brothers have all reached the NHL in recent years. Eric Staal is a top scorer who led Carolina to the Stanley Cup in 2006. Jordan is a two-way talent who helped Pittsburgh win the Cup in 2009 before joining Eric in Carolina for the 2012–13 season. Late that year, Jared Staal was called up from the minors and played on a line with his Eric and Jordan when he made his NHL debut with the Hurricanes on April 25, 2013. Carolina's opponent that night was the New York Rangers, who featured defenseman Marc Staal, though he was out of action that night due to an injury.

The Case for the Defense

Though their primary job is to protect their goaltender, defensemen who can also score get most of the glory. Bobby Orr of Boston revolutionized the position in the 1960s and '70s. No one ever combined these roles better than him and the image of his 1970 Stanley Cup-winning goal is one of hockey's most famous.

Because his son was rather small for his age, Doug Orr wanted his boy Bobby to be a forward. However, former NHL defenseman Bucko McDonald, who coached the young prodigy in his hometown of Parry Sound, Ontario, thought Bobby Orr had the makings of a great defenseman. McDonald encouraged Orr to use his offensive skills, but he also taught him the finer points of playing defense. NHL scouts soon took note.

When Orr was just 14 years old, the Boston Bruins worked out an arrangement with his family that allowed him to play junior hockey with the Oshawa Generals. Orr lived at home that whole season. He had no opportunity to practice with his team and he played against young men as old as 21. Still, he was good enough to be named a second-team all-star. After four stellar seasons with the Generals, an 18-year-old Orr was of age to enter the NHL.

Despite a knee injury that forced him out for three weeks (and would plague him throughout his career), Orr was easily the most exciting new performer of 1966–67 and an instant fan favorite in Boston. He not only choreographed the Bruins offense, but was its spearhead with his whirling rushes. Orr had 13 goals and 41 points, (second only to Chicago's Pierre Pilote among NHL defensemen), was awarded the Calder Trophy as rookie of the year, and was named to the Second All-Star Team. He was not the first defenseman to direct his team's attack, but his immense skill in doing so changed the way hockey was played.

Bobby Orr also ushered in hockey's new economic age, retaining Toronto lawyer Alan Eagleson to act as his agent in the negotiation of his first contract with the Bruins in 1966. Bruins general manager Hap Emms had offered Orr a standard rookie contract: an annual salary of $8,000 plus a $5,000 bonus. Orr and his agent stood firm, and eventually negotiated a two-year contract worth $75,000. It was a staggering amount of money at the time, but Orr proved he was more than worth it.

Beginning in his second season of 1967–68, Orr won the Norris Trophy and was selected to the First All-Star Team for eight consecutive years. He set a record for defensemen when he scored 21 goals in 1968–69, then smashed it with 33 goals the following year when he also became the first defenseman to top 100 points and win the NHL scoring title. In the playoffs, Orr scored the Stanley Cup-winning goal in overtime as the Bruins became NHL champions for the first time since 1941. He won both the Hart Trophy as NHL MVP and the Conn Smythe Trophy as playoff MVP that year, and went on to become the first player in NHL history to win the Hart Trophy three years in a row. He won the Conn Smythe Trophy again when Boston won the Stanley Cup in 1972. In 1970–71, Orr set a new NHL record (later broken

by Wayne Gretzky) with 102 assists. His 139 points that year remain a record for defensemen. He won a second scoring title with 135 points in 1974–75. Sadly, Orr never played another full season after that 1974–75 campaign. Knee injuries limited him to just 36 games over the next four years and forced his retirement in November of 1978.

Orr's brilliance overshadowed contemporaries like Brad Park, but his early retirement cast a greater light on players like Denis Potvin and Larry

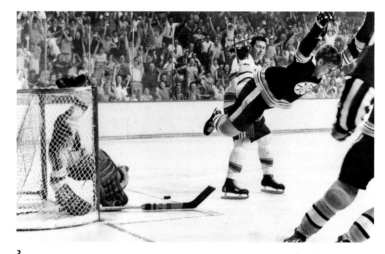

1: Bobby Orr starred for four seasons with the Oshawa Generals en route to NHL superstardom.

2: The family of James Norris, late owner of the Detroit Red Wings, donated the Norris Trophy to the NHL in 1954.

3: Orr is sent flying as he celebrates his Stanley Cup-winning goal for the Bruins in 1970.

4: Raymond Bourque followed in the footsteps of Eddie Shore and Bobby Orr on the Boston defense.

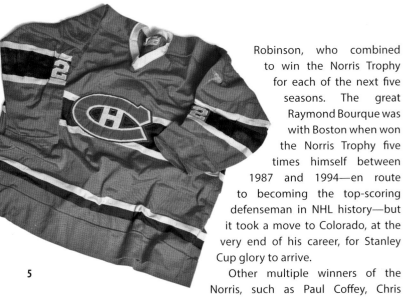

Robinson, who combined to win the Norris Trophy for each of the next five seasons. The great Raymond Bourque was with Boston when won the Norris Trophy five times himself between 1987 and 1994—en route to becoming the top-scoring defenseman in NHL history—but it took a move to Colorado, at the very end of his career, for Stanley Cup glory to arrive.

Other multiple winners of the Norris, such as Paul Coffey, Chris Chelios and Nicklas Lidstrom, have all ranked among the top-scoring defensemen in each of their Trophy-winning seasons, as have one-time winners Randy Carlyle, Doug Wilson, Brian Leetch, Rob Blake, Al MacInnis, Chris Pronger and Erik Karlsson. In fact, since the Norris Trophy was donated to honor the league's best blueliner back in 1954, the only truly defensive defenseman to win it was Rod Langway, who won it with the Washington Capitals in 1982–83 and 1983–84.

Doug Harvey

Doug Harvey was the best defenseman in hockey during his heyday, and ranks with Bobby Orr and Eddie Shore among the greatest of all time. His ability to check, block shots, rush the puck, stickhandle and pass allowed him to control the pace of the game.

After a lengthy amateur career in his hometown of Montreal, Harvey entered the NHL with the Canadiens in 1947–48. By his fifth season, it was apparent he was among the best in the game. He earned his first All-Star selection in 1951–52 and would be chosen for 11 straight years. In 10 of those 11 years, Harvey was selected as a First Team All-Star. He also won the Norris Trophy seven times in eight years between 1955 and 1962, missing out in 1958–59 when the award went to teammate Tom Johnson. Harvey played on Stanley Cup winners in Montreal in 1953 and in every year from 1956 to 1960.

When hockey began, it was a game that developed in "straight-ahead, straight-line playing patterns," wrote Ken Dryden in *The Game*. Defenders were often awkward skaters—but they had the time to react to the limited set of options that attackers possessed. However, the rise of the speed and transition games changed that. In a swift game with ever-changing patterns, it becomes crucial for a defender to learn to make calm but instant decisions.

Whether offensively gifted or defensively sound, vision and awareness are keys to success for all defensemen. It's the blueliners with the best vision who get to enjoy the most playing time. Given that every NHL defender needs a fair share of size, speed and skill nowadays, vision is arguably the most important trait they can have. And there are no statistics to measure that!

5: Sweater worn by Jacques Laperriere, who won the Stanley Cup five times with Montreal and the Norris Trophy in 1966.

6: Ottawa superstar defenseman Erik Karlsson is a three-time First Team NHL All-Star and a winner of the Norris Trophy on two occasions.

7: Denis Potvin of the New York Islanders was offensively gifted and tough on defense.

Hockey's Greatest Rivalries

Whether it's the Leafs vs. Canadiens, the Oilers vs. Flames, or the Rangers vs. Islanders, certain matchups capture fans' imaginations. History and geography play a big part in sports rivalries and hockey has had more than its fair share—dating back to long before the birth of the NHL.

1

Throughout its history, the National Hockey League has seen a great many classic rivalries. Some of the best date back to the Original Six years of 1942 to 1967. Yet rivalries were heating up the ice long before there was an NHL.

No matter what the era, Montreal seems to be at the center of so many great hockey rivalries. Though it was the success of the Ottawa Hockey Club in 1892 that convinced Lord Stanley to donate the Stanley Cup, it was Montreal that dominated the trophy's early years. By the time Ottawa finally won the Cup in 1903, Montreal teams had claimed eight of the first ten championships. When Ottawa's run ended in 1906, it was the Montreal Wanderers that beat them.

The Ottawa Senators battled with the Wanderers and the Montreal Canadiens throughout the existence of the National Hockey Association. The rivalry with the Canadiens extended through the birth of the NHL. From 1916 through 1925, when Stanley Cup battles pitted the eastern champs against the best of the western leagues, either the Canadiens or the Senators reached the Stanley Cup Final eight times in ten seasons and combined to win five titles. When the Senators finally began to decline in

the late 1920s, the Canadiens didn't have to look far for a new rival. In fact, by the 1926–27 season, they were sharing a building with them.

The Montreal Forum had been built for the Montreal Maroons when

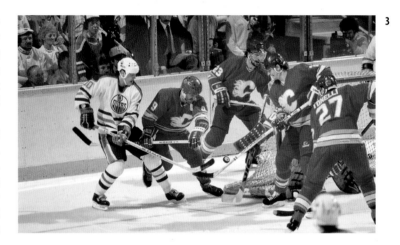

3

1: Nels Stewart of the Montreal Maroons.

2: The Maple Leafs versus the Canadiens remains one of the NHL's most fervent rivalries.

3: Calgary's Lanny McDonald tries to keep Edmonton's Esa Tikkanen away from the puck in a goalmouth scramble during one of the 1986 editions of the Battle of Alberta.

they entered the NHL in 1924. The Canadiens were defending Stanley Cup champions then, but only one year later, the Maroons won the Cup. Clearly, both teams were talented. Add to this mix the French–English element—the Maroons were English Montreal's team, the Canadiens the French team—and all the pieces were in place for a bitter rivalry.

During the 1930s, the Toronto Maple Leafs probably had a bigger rivalry with the Maroons than they had with the Canadiens. The Leafs–Canadiens rivalry didn't really heat up until the 1940s when Frank Selke left Conn Smythe's employ in Toronto to begin building dynasties in Montreal. Between 1938 and 1970, the Leafs and the Canadiens were the NHL's only Canadian teams. Naturally they attracted (and bitterly divided!) fans from all across the country. Still, the rivalry was rooted in the cities themselves. One was English and Protestant, the other French and Catholic.

Toronto and Montreal competed in business and finance, but people considered the city of Toronto dull and workmanlike, while Montreal was vibrant and emotional. The Leafs and Canadiens seemed to reflect these values, and both did so successfully. Toronto's grinders dominated the 1940s NHL, and Montreal's Flying Frenchmen the 1950s (when their rivalry with the Detroit Red Wings as every bit as fierce as any in hockey history). In the 1960s, both teams won the Stanley Cup four times.

Though there is still nothing in the NHL like a Saturday night in Toronto or Montreal when the Leafs or Canadiens come to town, the rivalry has never really been the same since the NHL expanded in 1967. (In the early 2000s, Ottawa became Toronto's biggest rival, though the Battle of Ontario

New York, New York (Part II)

After the demise of the New York Americans, the Rangers had the local hockey scene pretty much to themselves for 30 years until the NHL added an expansion team on Long Island in 1972. The Rangers beat their expansion rivals in all six meetings in 1972–73, and outscored them 25–5.

The tables were turned just two seasons later when the Islanders ousted the Rangers in the 1975 playoffs. The Rangers returned this favor in 1979, eliminating the Islanders in a six-game semifinal series. For the next 10 years, the Islanders had the upper hand. From 1980 to 1983, the Islanders won the Stanley Cup four years in a row, knocking out the Rangers en route in each of the last three seasons. Until the Rangers finally ended their championship drought in 1994, Islanders fans would chant "19–40!" at their rivals in a mocking reference to the fact the Broadway Blueshirts had not won the Stanley Cup since then.

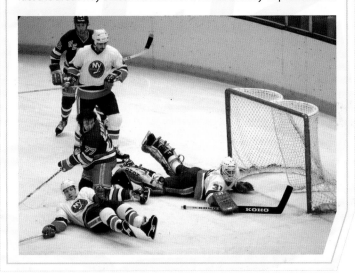

4: The New York Americans were first to arrive in The Big Apple, but the star-spangled squad soon played second fiddle to the New York Rangers.

5: Tickets to a Saturday night game between the Toronto Maple Leafs and the Montreal Canadiens are always a prized possession.

6: Much has been made of the rivalry between today's high-scoring superstars, Washington's Alex Ovechkin (#8) and Pittsburgh's Sidney Crosby (#87)

was oddly lopsided with the Senators dominating the regular-season meetings, but the Maple Leafs coming out on top in the playoffs.)

During the 1970s, the Canadiens found their biggest rivals in Boston. Both teams ranked among the best in the NHL throughout the decade, but the Canadiens almost always came out on top—particularly in the playoffs. Montreal stunned a power-packed Boston team in a 1971 quarterfinal series, and then beat them again in the Stanley Cup Final in 1977 and 1978. Montreal's win in the 1979 semifinals was another classic. When the Bruins finally beat the Canadiens in the playoffs in 1988, it marked their first win in 18 matchups dating back to 1943!

During the 1980s, the Canadiens once again found their biggest rival in their own backyard. In 1979, the Quebec Nordiques joined the NHL from the World Hockey Association, and by 1981–82 "The Battle of Quebec" emerged as a premier NHL matchup. While the Habs and Nordiques were fighting for the honor of *la belle province*, the Calgary Flames and Edmonton Oilers were waging "The Battle of Alberta" in the Canadian west.

Like Toronto and Montreal, residents of Calgary and Edmonton have been rivals on and off the ice, with business, politics, culture and football dividing citizens for decades. In the NHL, the Flames and (especially) the Oilers dominated the Stanley Cup in the 1980s. In fact, one of those two teams played in the Final for eight straight seasons from 1983 until 1990, with the Oilers winning the Cup in 1984, 1985, 1987, 1988 and 1990, and the Flames winning in 1989. It was a pretty good bet that whichever one of those two teams survived what seemed to be their annual playoff battle in the old Smythe Division was going to wind up sipping champagne come season's end.

Famous Coaches

Once all the best coaches were former stars. Today many of the men who patrol behind the benches have never played in the NHL or they were former journeymen players who had to be keen students of hockey just to hang on to their spots on the roster.

1

It has long been said that coaches are hired to be fired, or that it's easier to fire a coach than it is to fire 20 players. Once upon a time though, a coach's job with his NHL team was much more secure than that of any but the game's most exalted star players. From the beginning of their coaching careers in the 1920s, legendary names like Art Ross in Boston, Lester Patrick in New York, and Jack Adams in Detroit, held their coaching positions for years… aided by the fact they were also long-time general managers! From 1940 to 1968, the Montreal Canadiens had just two coaches: Dick Irvin and Toe Blake. During their combined tenures the Canadiens finished first in the regular season 11 times, won the Stanley Cup 11 times, and missed the playoffs only once.

Over the years, the path followed by coaches to the NHL has changed. In the pre-NHL years of Stanley Cup competition, teams almost always had a playing coach or a playing manager. Through the years many teams in amateur and minor pro hockey have employed playing coaches. There were even a few in the NHL until the late 1960s, though league rules today no longer allow for it. NHL playing coaches were always rare, but star players who became coaches were certainly not.

From the 1920s through the late 1960s dominant, long-time winning coaches like Adams, Patrick, Ross, Irvin and Blake all made it to the Hockey Hall of Fame on the basis of their playing careers. Since 1968, only three Hall of Fame players have coached Stanley Cup-winning teams: Tom Johnson with Boston in 1972, Jacques Lemaire with New Jersey in 1995 and Larry Robinson with the Devils in 2000. During that same 49-year span only six other Cup-winning coaches—Glen Sather, Al Arbour, Terry Crisp, Randy Carlyle, Joel Quenneville, Darryl Sutter, and Mike Sullivan—had what could considered lengthy NHL playing careers. The era of the "career coach" had arrived. In fact, from 1990 to 2016, 20 different men were Stanley Cup-winning coaches, but only eight of them—Lemaire, Robinson, Marc Crawford, Peter Laviolette, Carlyle, Dan Bylsma, Quenneville, Claude Julien, Sutter, and Sullivan—had ever played in the NHL, and Laviolette only played 12 games, while Julien played just 14. Scotty Bowman, John Muckler, Bob Johnson, Jacques Demers, Mike Keenan, Ken Hitchcock, Bob Hartley, Pat Burns, John Tortorella and Mike Babcock never played in the NHL. In fact, most of them never even played professional hockey!

As the only three-time winner of the Jack Adams Award as coach of the year, Pat Burns was certainly one of the most successful of the new breed of NHL coaches. A policeman by trade, Burns began coaching in minor hockey. He became head coach of the Hull Olympiques

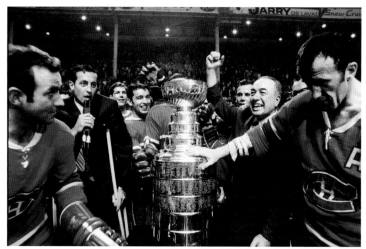

2 3

4

1: Bob Johnson earned this Stanley Cup ring as coach of the 1990–91 Pittsburgh Penguins.

2: Joel Quenneville played defense for six NHL teams before embarking on a coaching career that saw him win three Cups with the Blackhawks.

3: Lester Patrick was the coach and general manager of the Rangers, then just GM, from 1926 to 1947.

4: Montreal Canadiens coach Toe Blake celebrated eight Stanley Cup championships between 1956 and 1968.

5: Scotty Bowman coached nine Stanley Cup champions: five with Montreal, one with Pittsburgh and three with Detroit.

6: Roger Neilson introduced the NHL to videotape as a coaching tool.

7: Detroit Red Wings players gather around coach Mike Babcock to discuss strategy during a time out.

5

in the Quebec Major Junior Hockey League in 1983 while still working as a detective, and was encouraged to follow his hockey dreams by the team's part owner, Wayne Gretzky. Burns coached the Canadiens top farm club in 1987–88, and was in the NHL with the Montreal the following season. Popular and successful with the Canadiens, Maple Leafs and Bruins, Burns finally won the Stanley Cup with the New Jersey Devils in 2003.

More typical of the new coaching breed is Mike Babcock, who played hockey at McGill University, holds a bachelor's degree in physical education, and had a lengthy apprenticeship in junior hockey. Babcock is the only man to coach Canada to victory at the World Championships and the World Junior Championships, and also has two Olympic gold medals to go along with his 2008 Stanley Cup victory in Detroit.

Throughout the NHL's first six decades coaching was mainly a one-man show. This began to change in the early 1980s when teams started hiring assistant coaches. At first, having one assistant behind the bench was a novelty but their numbers increased as the NHL grew. Today most teams have many assistant coaches who have specific assignments. Some are former players, but others join NHL staffs after coaching careers at the college, junior, or minor pro level.

Head coaches in the past handled all player changes during a game, but many teams now have an assistant who changes defense pairings and another who changes forward lines. Another assistant is often getting a different view of the game from a location high in the arena. Most of the coaches in bygone years admitted they knew little about goaltending, unless they had been one in their playing days. Today, every organization has a goaltending coach who works with the netminders on the NHL team and with young prospects playing junior hockey or in minor pro leagues.

In earlier days the only time a coach saw his opponents was when his team was playing them. Today, most teams employ someone who

Al Arbour and Scotty Bowman

On November 3, 2007, former New York Islanders coach Al Arbour—pictured below—stepped behind the bench one final time. Current Islanders coach Ted Nolan (with the NHL's blessing) had arranged for Arbour to coach his 1,500th game with the franchise. At age 75, Arbour became the oldest coach in NHL history. With a 3–2 win over Pittsburgh that night, Arbour—who originally coached the team from 1973 to 1986, and again from 1988 to 1994—ran his Islanders record to 740–537–223 with four Stanley Cup victories.

Arbour's 740 Islanders victories are the most by any coach with a single team. However, his career total of 782 victories ranks a distant second to Scotty Bowman on the all-time list. Bowman had a record of 1,244–584–313 (in a record 2,141 games) in 30 years behind the bench with St. Louis, Montreal, Buffalo, Pittsburgh and Detroit. Bowman's 353 playoff games, 223 playoff wins and nine Stanley Cup victories are also NHL records.

has the job of recording games involving other teams, and then editing the resulting video to show their systems and tendencies on offense, defense, power-plays and penalty killing. It's hard to believe that when Roger Neilson began his NHL coaching career with the Toronto Maple Leafs in 1977, he was dubbed "Captain Video" and considered an eccentric for his habit of studying game tapes.

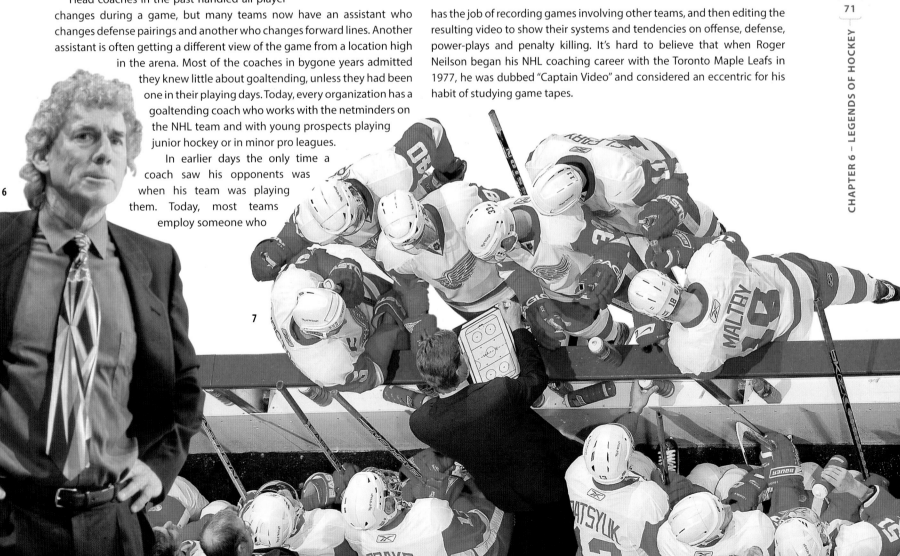

Chapter 7
Trophies and Awards

Every sport celebrates its winners—both teams and individuals—but none do it as well as the National Hockey League. The Stanley Cup, as well as being North America's oldest annually contested team trophy, may also be its most famous. Uniquely, every player from the winning team is entitled to own the Stanley Cup for one day and take it where they wish. As for individual glory, there are 14 different trophies presented at a special awards ceremony, celebrating everything from the best player to the one exhibiting the best sportsmanship and most gentlemanly conduct.

Chris Pronger won the Stanley Cup
with Anaheim Ducks in 2007.

Beginning in 1945, an organization in Kingston, Ontario, began inducting the finest players in the history of hockey, originally only who played in North America. An actual building finally opened in 1961, and the Hockey Hall of Fame has been based in Toronto ever since.

1

3

The roots of the Hockey Hall of Fame reach back to September 10, 1943, when the NHL and the Canadian Amateur Hockey Association approved a plan put forward by Kingston, Ontario's Captain James T. Sutherland. For many years, the Hall was based was Kingston, though it would eventually shift to Toronto.

The first inductions to the Hockey Hall of Fame were made in 1945. For years, 12 players have been listed as the original Hall of Famers, though, in fact, only nine were enshrined that year. Those nine men were Hobey Baker, Charlie Gardiner, Eddie Gerard, Frank McGee, Howie Morenz, Tom Phillips, Harvey Pulford, Hod Stuart and Georges Vezina. All nine were deceased, and only eight were supposed to be elected, but Baker and Pulford ended up tied in the voting. Sir H. Montagu Allan (donor of the Allan Cup) and Lord Stanley of Preston were added to the original list as builders.

Two years later, in 1947, Frank Calder, W.A. Hewitt, Francis Nelson, William Northey, John Ross Robertson, Claude Robinson and James Sutherland himself were all inducted as builders. The first class of living Hall of Fame players was also inducted that year, beginning with Dit Clapper (who was

inducted immediately upon ending his 20-year career with the Boston Bruins) and including Aurel Joliat, Frank Nighbor, Lester Patrick, Eddie Shore, Cyclone Taylor and Russell "Dubbie" Bowie—wrongly credited as a 1945 induction. Dan Bain and Art Ross, also incorrectly attributed with 1945 inductions, were elected to the Hall of Fame in 1949.

After more elections in 1950 and 1952, the Hall of Fame named no new members until 1958, and elections became annual after 1959. The Hall of Fame building was finally opened in 1961 on the grounds of Toronto's Canadian National Exhibition.

The Hockey Hall of Fame became a Toronto landmark

$300,000 Hockey Hall Of

Hockey is to have a "Hall of Fame" in a new $300,000 structure to be built in Exhibition Park this winter.

The hockey hall of fame, for several years a pet project of H. I. Price, president of the CNE, is included in the city's capital budget that board of control is weighing. At first sight the item of $300,000 looks inappropriate when other expenditures of more intrinsic public value are being cut off; for instance, $250,000 for planned ravine land purchases. Was the National Hockey league not supposed to foot the bill for the new hall of fame?

That is still the intention, apparently, and taxpayers would be putting up very little of the cost. The city may borrow the $300,000 now, so that work can be-

gin. The NHL will struction costs in sev instalments, but will the carrying charge

This arrangemen provided it is spelle legal agreement an or to the fluctuatin hockey league. T tributing quite eno land, covering the charges and proba paying annual Council must en people will in fact

The CNE will at small public co will get a permar national game.

2

4

5

1: Mark Messier's Hall of Fame career saw Stanley Cup Final wins with the Edmonton Oilers and New York Rangers.

2: Jean Beliveau retired as a 10-time Stanley Cup champion after the 1970–71 season and was elected to the Hall of Fame in 1972.

3: A newspaper story details the Hall's construction costs.

4: The first Hockey Hall of Fame officially opened on August 26, 1961. The building also housed Canada's Sports Hall of Fame.

5: Construction of the original Hockey Hall of Fame building on the grounds of Toronto's Canadian National Exhibition.

and its first curators, Bobby Hewitson (1961 to 1967) and Lefty Reid (1967 to 1988), acquired such a huge collection of memorabilia that the Hall outgrew its original home. In 1986, former NHL referee-in-chief Scotty Morrison was named the Hall's chairman. His mandate: Find a new venue for the Hockey Hall of Fame.

On June 18, 1993, the Hockey Hall of Fame officially opened its new home at BCE Place (now Brookfield Place) in downtown Toronto. More than 500,000 people attended the new Hockey Hall of Fame in its first year. Exhibits display the entire history of the sport from minor hockey to international games, and in keeping with the Hall's mandate to continually change and add new features, major expansions and renovations took place in 1998 and 2006.

A designated charity, the Hall of Fame strives to educate and entertain while promoting excellence at every level of the game. Behind the scenes, the Hall maintains an ambitious resource center that has become a world leader in scholarship and research about the sport. In addition, hockey fans from all over the world donate items to the Hall's archival collection. These donations range from sweaters to scrapbooks, programs to photographs and trophies to ticket stubs. Several of these donated items are depicted in this book.

A Selection Committee, whose 18 members include ex-players, media representatives and hockey executives, elect each new Hall of Fame member in a vote announced in July. Inductions are held in November. The Selection Committee chooses members in three categories: Players, Builders and Referees/Linesmen. Candidates for election as Honoured Members in the player category are chosen the basis of their playing ability, sportsmanship, character and their contribution to their team or teams and to the game of hockey in general. Candidates in the other categories are judged by similar criteria.

To be eligible for induction, a player must be retired for three years (though Gordie Howe, Guy Lafleur and Mario Lemieux all "unretired" after being elected to the Hall and actually played in the NHL as active Hall of Famers.) Over the years, 10 star players have been exempted from the three-year waiting period: Dit Clapper, Maurice Richard, Ted Lindsay,

Hall of Fame Voting

Up to six (maximum of four male, two female) players along with two builders and/or referee/linesmen can be inducted into the Hockey Hall of Fame every year. Each member of the Selection Committee is allowed to nominate one candidate in each of the categories. As long as at least 10 members of the Committee are on hand at the annual meeting, an election can take place. Each vote is carried out by secret ballot.

Voters can choose up to the maximum number of candidates on their ballot. Any candidate receiving at least 75 percent approval is declared elected. Candidates receiving fewer than 50 percent of the votes are dropped from further consideration for the year in question. If the maximum number of candidates is not elected on the first ballot, a series of run-off ballots are cast. No further votes are cast if no one reaches 75 percent.

8

Red Kelly, Terry Sawchuk, Jean Beliveau, Gordie Howe, Bobby Orr, Mario Lemieux and Wayne Gretzky. After Gretzky's induction in 1999 the rules for induction were changed to ensure that the three-year waiting period would become mandatory for all players.

In 2010, for the first time, two female players—Angela James and Cammi Granato—were inducted into the Hall of Fame. Geraldine Heaney was inducted in 2014 and, in 2016, Angela Ruggiero became the fourth female inductee.

6: The entryway to the NHL Zone at the Hockey Hall of Fame.

7: Memorabilia on display in the Hall's World of Hockey.

8: Captain James T. Sutherland, the driving force behind the establishment of the Hockey Hall of Fame.

9: Former Oilers and Rangers captain Mark Messier speaks

during the 2007 Hall of Fame Inductions.

10: This souvenir key ring displays the old bank building that is the heart of the new Hockey Hall of Fame.

6

7

9

10

The Summit Series and Beyond

Canada dominated the Olympic hockey competition from the 1920s to the early 1950s, but then the Soviet Union rose to power. Canadians always believed their best professionals could beat the Russians and they finally got a chance in 1972 when the Canada–Russia Summit Series opened the door for top-level international tournaments.

For years, the best amateur teams in Canada easily dominated international hockey. From 1920 to 1952, Canada earned gold medals in six of seven Olympic tournaments—Great Britain, with mainly Canadian players, won in 1936—and won 16 of 19 World Championship tournaments. But on March 7, 1954, a new era in international hockey began.

The 1954 World Championship marked the debut of the Soviet Union on the international hockey stage. They were more than ready to compete, running up a 5–0–1 record through their first six games of the round robin tournament. The Canadians, represented by the Junior B East York Lyndhursts, outscored their opposition 57–5 in winning each of their first six games. A crowd of 17,000 witnessed the first meeting between Canada and the Soviet Union in the final game on March 7. The newcomers jumped out to a 4–0 first-period lead and went on to win the game—and the World title—by a score of 7–2.

The Soviets used strong skating and a short passing game to claim their first World Championship. It was a combination that became all too familiar to their opponents when the Soviets dominated international competition in the 1960s. Canada, which abandoned the use of club teams for a national team program in 1964, was still forced to use amateur talent against Soviet players who were, if not technically professionals, certainly full time hockey players. Canadian fans longed to see a series that would pit the best Canadian professionals against the best the Soviets had to offer. In September of 1972, they got their wish.

Most Canadians expected the 1972 Summit Series to be a one-sided romp for the NHL's best players. When the Soviets posted a 7–3 victory in the opening game in Montreal, the nation was stunned. Coach Harry Sinden shuffled his lineup for game two in Toronto and the result was a 4–1 Canadian victory, but Soviet goalie Vladislav Tretiak was magnificent in a 4–4 tie in game three at Winnipeg. Game

four saw Team Canada take several careless penalties en route to a 5–3 loss. Canada's rugged style appeared graceless next to the smooth skating and slick passing of the Soviets and fans in Vancouver booed the Canadians loudly. After the game, Phil Esposito made an emotional plea for support on national television. The 3,000 Canadian fans that followed the team to Moscow did not let him down.

Though Team Canada dropped its first game in Russia, they stormed back to win games six and seven to even the series. Few Canadians who were alive on September 28, 1972 missed game eight. Absenteeism was high at work places across the country and schools suspended classes to allow students to watch. They saw Team Canada overcome bad refereeing

1: A ticket stub from Game 8 of the Summit Series in Moscow, September 28, 1972.

2: Paul Henderson scored the winning goal in each of the final three games of the 1972 Summit Series.

3: Prime Minister Pierre Trudeau opened the 1972 Summit Series.

4: The 1954 Soviet national team launched a new era, winning the IIHF World Championship in their debut appearance.

5: Soviet winger Valeri Kharlamov dazzled fans with his speed and skills in 1972. Here he checks defenseman Brad Park.

6: A spectacular goal by Pete Mahovlich helped Team Canada salvage some pride with a 4–1 win in game two of the Summit Series.

7: The Canada Cup trophy. The original in 1976 was made of solid nickel and weighed 125 pounds. Replicas built in 1981 and 1984 are housed at the Hockey Hall of Fame.

8: A souvenir pin from the 1972 Series.

and a 5–3 deficit to rally for a thrilling 6–5 victory on a Paul Henderson goal with just 34 seconds left to play.

Now that the appetite for best-on-best international hockey had been whetted, there was no looking back. The Olympics were still barred to professional athletes, so alternative tournaments had to be created. In 1976, the Canada Cup was introduced, pitting the top players from Canada, Russia, Czechoslovakia, Sweden, Finland and the United States against each other in a six-team tournament.

Created by the NHL, the NHL Players Association and Hockey Canada, the Canada Cup heralded Canada's official return to international hockey after a boycott that began in 1970. Team Canada's roster boasted one of the strongest lineups ever assembled, including Bobby Orr and Bobby Hull, who had missed the 1972 Canada–Russia Summit Series (Orr due to injuries and Hull because he had left the NHL for the World Hockey Association). The roster also included Phil Esposito, Guy Lafleur, Gilbert Perreault and Denis Potvin. Orr, who enjoyed a final turn in the spotlight before repeated knee injuries ended his brilliant career, was the MVP of the 1976 Canada Cup, but it was Darryl Sittler who scored a thrilling tournament-winning goal in overtime versus Czechoslovakia.

In the 1981 Canada Cup, the Soviets scored a shocking 8–1 win over Canada in the final, but Canada came out on top in the 1984, 1987 and 1991 tournaments. When the tournament became the World Cup of Hockey, it was won by the United States in 1996 and by Canada in 2004 and 2016.

In addition to these national team tournaments, various "Super Series" of midseason exhibition games were played in North American arenas between Soviet club teams and NHL teams from 1975–76 through 1990–91. Also, the NHL All-Star Game was twice replaced by special international events during this time. In February 1979, the Soviet national team defeated the NHL All-Stars in a three-game series at Madison Square Garden in New York and won a trophy named the Challenge Cup. There was no winner at the two-game Rendez-Vous '87 series in Quebec City after the Soviets and the NHL All-Stars each won one game.

The Miracle on Ice

Herb Brooks had been the last player cut from the 1960 U.S. squad that won a surprising gold medal at the Squaw Valley Winter Olympics. In 1980, he coached an unknown assortment of American college kids to the Olympics in Lake Placid. Team USA was 42–14–3 in the first 59 games of their pre-Olympic schedule, but were hammered 10–3 by the Soviet national team in their final tune-up.

The Americans rallied to tie Sweden 2–2 in their first Olympic game then got on a roll, beating Czechoslovakia, Norway, Romania and West Germany with stellar goaltending from Jim Craig and an offense led by Mark Johnson. Next was a medal-round rematch with the Soviets. The Americans were outshot 39–16, yet captain Mike Eruzione rallied them to a 4–3 victory. But the "Miracle on Ice" would not truly be complete without a victory in the final game. When the Americans beat Finland 4–2, the gold medal was theirs.

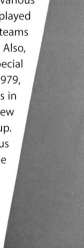

7

8

On the Trail of the Stanley Cup

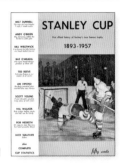

No trophy has collected more air miles than the Stanley Cup. Since 1993, every member of the winning team gets to have it for a day, whether it means going to Montreal, Miami or Moscow. Lord Stanley's gift to hockey has found itself in a wide variety of places.

1

Many things about the Stanley Cup have changed since the days of the late Victorian era: Teams no longer challenge the champion; Series are scheduled in June, not January; Players get paid to fight for it. Even the trophy itself has grown from a simple, squat bowl into a shining silver tower.

Some things about the Stanley Cup, however, remain timeless. The hockey players from the Montreal AAA were presented with the first Stanley Cup commemorative rings in 1893. The Winnipeg Victorias held the first Stanley Cup parade in 1896, and were the first players to drink champagne from the bowl. Back then, though, individual players on the winning team were not given their own special day to spend with the Stanley Cup. This modern NHL tradition began in 1993, the year of the Cup's centennial.

Previous to 1993, the Stanley Cup would make brief appearances at team parties and might occasionally show up at a few other official functions. Sometimes it might be "borrowed" by a player, such as Montreal Canadiens superstar Guy Lafleur, who once spirited the Cup away to his parents' home in Thurso, Quebec, or by members of the Edmonton Oilers, who would appear with the Cup at various locations around town during their Cup dynasty of the 1980s. But in honor of the Stanley Cup's 100th birthday, each member of the 1992–93 champion Montreal Canadiens was permitted to take the Cup home with him. This decision proved to be a very popular one with players and fans alike.

Though everyone did not get his own special day with the Stanley Cup in 1994, when the New York Rangers won it that year for the first time since 1940, giddy players took it on a tour of the Big Apple and environs the likes of which the old trophy had never seen! The Cup went to Belmont Park, where stories say it was filled with oats and served to Kentucky Derby winner Go For Gin; it went to Yankee Stadium; it visited

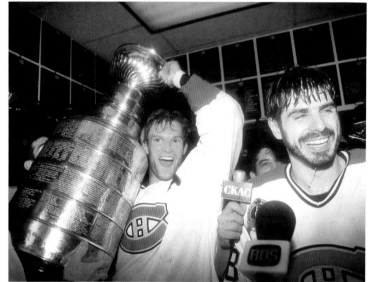

3

1: *History of the Stanley Cup* cover from 1957.

2: The original Stanley Cup bowl is preserved in Plexiglas at the Hockey Hall of Fame in Toronto.

3: Kirk Muller and J.J. Daigneault would each get their own day with the Stanley Cup in the summer of 1993.

4: Chris Pronger celebrates with the Stanley Cup in Anaheim in 2007.

2

5: Phil Pritchard rests beside a VIP passenger on a flight to Moscow in 1997.

6: Mike Bolt of the Hockey Hall of Fame spends much of each summer with Stanley.

7: Viachelsav Fetisov, Igor Larionov and Vyacheslav Kozlov celebrate Detroit's Stanley Cup victory in Moscow in the summer of 1997.

countless bars and restaurants; and it has fallen out of the back of at least one car.

When the NHL decided in 1995 that the idea of giving each winning team member their own day with the Stanley Cup should become an annual tradition, it was also decided that a staff member from the Hockey Hall of Fame—one of a group now known collectively as "The Keepers of the Cup"—would accompany the trophy at all times. Since then, the Cup's adventures have taken it all over the world.

The first trip to Europe came when Peter Forsberg took the Stanley Cup to Sweden after the Colorado Avalanche won it in 1996. In 1997, the Cup went to Russia with several members of the Detroit Red Wings. Since then, there have been trips to Finland, the Czech Republic, Switzerland and various former Soviet republics.

In North America, the Cup has visited the Parliament Buildings in Ottawa, the White House in Washington, an Inuit igloo in Rankin Inlet, mountaintops in the Rockies, beaches in California and parties with Hollywood celebrities. It has helped to deliver engagement rings and to christen newborn babies. After the Carolina Hurricanes' victory in 2006, Glen Wesley took the Stanley Cup to visit wounded U.S. Marines at nearby Camp Lejeune. In the spring of 2007, a group of 17 former NHL players took the Cup to visit Canadian soldiers and other NATO forces who were serving in Afghanistan.

The Cup that travels with the players in the summer (and makes charity appearances and NHL promotional trips throughout the hockey season) is always the same Cup that is presented to the teams on the ice after the final game. It's what the NHL and the Hockey Hall of Fame refer to as The Presentation Cup. Though it no longer includes Lord Stanley's original bowl (which was retired in 1970 after a duplicate was prepared in 1968), it IS the real Stanley Cup. To ensure that there is always something on display for Hall of Fame visitors, a replica of the Stanley Cup (and of all the other NHL trophies) was created in 1993. Lord Stanley's bowl and various other original bands and rings are on permanent display there.

For well over a century, the Stanley Cup has been hockey's talisman, a focal point shared by players and fans alike. Traveling almost 100,000 miles per year these days, the shimmering silver trophy has been displayed everywhere from Miami to Moscow and has been admired and photographed by hundreds of thousands of fans. It's been the star of the show at small-town arenas and on late-night talk shows, all the while conveying the pride and joy of having reached hockey's pinnacle.

The Keepers of the Cup

Since starring in a 2001 MasterCard commercial, Hockey Hall of Fame vice president and curator Phil Pritchard is the best-known member of "The Keepers of the Cup." Pritchard has been accompanying the Stanley Cup on its rounds since joining the Hall of Fame staff in 1988. Every year, he and colleague Craig Campbell, sporting their blue blazers and white gloves, carry the Stanley Cup onto the ice for presentation to the NHL champions.

In addition to Pritchard and Campbell, three other Hall of Fame staff members are currently responsible for safeguarding the Stanley Cup when it travels (as it does approximately 200 days of the year). Both Mike Bolt and Walt Neubrand began working at the Hall of Fame in 1995, and have been accompanying the Stanley Cup since 1997. The newest keeper is Howie Borrow.

Learning the history of the NHL's postseason award winners is a history lesson unto itself. The Stanley Cup is one of four team awards, the others going to the two Conference winners and the team registering the most points in the standings. As for individual trophies, it is not so simple. There is the MVP, Rookie of the Year ... plus another dozen.

Befitting of a league whose championship trophy is named for a British lord who became the Governor General of Canada, the NHL's annual individual awards are all named for various people—ranging from government officials to former players and team executives. "Just the names of the awards make them very unique," said NHL Network analyst E.J. Hradek. "It adds to the pride and tradition of the game that goes back many, many decades. Hart, Ross, Selke ... these are the builders and giants of the game."

There's even one trophy—the Lady Byng—named in honor of the wife of another former Governor General of Canada (Lord Byng held the post between 1921 and 1926). What's more unusual, the Lady Byng Trophy is awarded for sportsmanship.

"That's more of a throwback," said Hradek. "That's definitely not something you see in any of the other sports."

Here's a rundown of the major NHL awards and their origins:

Hart Memorial Trophy
Regular season league MVP. The original Hart Trophy was donated to the NHL in 1923 by Dr. David A. Hart, father of Cecil Hart, former manager-coach of the Montreal Canadiens. Wayne Gretzky won the award a record nine times during his career, including eight in a row from 1980–87.

Calder Memorial Trophy
Rookie of the year. While a rookie of the year has been awarded since 1937, it was named for former NHL President Frank Calder after his death in 1943.

James Norris Memorial Trophy
Top defenseman. The trophy was presented in 1953 by the four children of the late James Norris in memory of the former owner-president of the Detroit Red Wings. Bobby Orr of the Boston Bruins won the award for a record eight consecutive seasons (1968–75).

2

1: Wayne Gretzky with the Hart Memorial Trophy, an award he won a record nine times.

2: Sidney Crosby was the playoff MVP after Pittsburgh won the Stanley Cup in 2016.

3: Dominik Hasek was one of hockey's finest goaltenders for more than 15 years and won the Vezina Trophy six times.

4: Bobby Orr (right) with the Norris Trophy in 1970 Joining Orr are Phil Esposito (left) and Clarence S. Campbell.

3

5: Frank J. Selke was with the Toronto Maple Leafs from 1929 to 1946 and Montreal Canadiens 1946–64. The award in his honor goes to the NHL's best defensive forward.

6: Lady Byng (right) first presented the trophy to the player "adjudged to have exhinited the best tipe of sportsmanship and gentlemanly conduct" in 1925, when her husband Lord Byng was Governor General of Canada.

5

6

Vezina Trophy

Top goalkeeper. Three former owners of the Montreal Canadiens presented the trophy to the league in 1926–27 in memory of Georges Vezina, an outstanding goalkeeper for the Canadiens who collapsed during a game in 1925 and died of tuberculosis a few months later. Until the 1981–82 season, the Vezina Trophy was a statistical award given to the goalkeeper who allowed the fewest goals during the regular season. Billy Smith of the New York Islanders was the first winner of the Vezina after a vote by the Professional Hockey Writers Association decided who received the award. Jacques Plante won the most Vezinas—seven of them—one more than Dominik Hasek, who has the most under the current system of selection.

Ted Lindsay Award

"Most outstanding player," as voted by members of the NHL Players' Association. The award was first presented after the 1971–72 season. It honors Hall of Famer Ted Lindsay, an all-star forward who helped establish the original Players' Association. Comparable to the Hart Memorial Trophy, there are 13 players who have won both trophies in the same season: Guy Lafleur, Wayne Gretzky, Mario Lemieux, Mark Messier, Brett Hull, Sergei Fedorov, Eric Lindros, Dominik Hasek, Jaromir Jagr, Joe Sakic, Martin St. Louis, Sidney Crosby and Alexander Ovechkin.

Bill Masterton Memorial Trophy

Under the trusteeship of the Professional Hockey Writers' Association, this is given to the NHL player who best exemplifies the qualities of perseverance, sportsmanship and dedication to hockey. A grant from the PHWA is awarded annually to the Bill Masterton Scholarship Fund, based in Bloomington, Minn., in the name of the winner. The trophy was presented by the PHWA in 1968 in honor of the late William Masterton, a Minnesota North Stars player who died on January 15, 1968, from a head injury sustained during a game.

Frank J. Selke Trophy

Best defensive forward. The trophy was first awarded at the end of the 1977–78 NHL season. It was named after Frank J. Selke, former general manager of the Toronto Maple Leafs and Montreal Canadiens. Bob Gainey of the Canadiens won the trophy in each of the first four years it was given, and to date he has won it more times than any other player.

King Clancy Trophy

Player who best exemplifies leadership qualities on and off the ice and has made a noteworthy humanitarian contribution in his community. The Clancy Trophy was first presented to the NHL by the Board of Governors in 1988 to honor the late Francis M. "King" Clancy, a former Ottawa Senators and Toronto Maple Leafs player, as well as coach and general manager. Clancy was part of Toronto's first Stanley Cup-winning team in 1932.

Lady Byng Memorial Trophy

Player "adjudged to have exhibited the best type of sportsmanship and gentlemanly conduct" combined with a high standard of playing ability. Lady Byng, wife of Canada's Governor-General at the time, presented the Lady Byng Trophy in 1925. After Frank Boucher of the New York Rangers won the award seven times in eight seasons, he was given the trophy to keep and Lady Byng donated another trophy in 1936.

Jack Adams Award

Coach of the year. The award was presented by the NHL Broadcasters' Association in 1974 to commemorate the late Jack Adams, former coach and general manager of the Detroit Red Wings. Jacques Demers, 1986–87 and 1987–88, is the only coach to win the award in consecutive seasons—as the Red Wings' coach, whereas Pat Burns is the only coach to win the Jack Adams Award three times, while four coaches have won the award with two different teams.

William M. Jennings Trophy

The goalkeeper with the fewest goals allowed (minimum, 25 games). Until 1981–82, the Vezina Trophy was awarded on this merit. When the Vezina became a subjective award, the NHL incorporated the Jennings Trophy. The Jennings Trophy honors the late William M. Jennings, longtime governor and president of the New York Rangers and one of the great builders of hockey in the United States. A total of six goaltenders have won both the Jennings and Vezina trophies in the same season. In addition to Miikka Kiprusoff and Tim Thomas, four others have won both trophies on at least two separate occasions: Patrick Roy, Martin Brodeur, Ed Belfour and Dominik Hasek. Brodeur and Roy have won or shared the award five times each.

Maurice Richard Trophy

Top goal scorer in the regular season. The trophy, first presented in 1999, was a gift to the NHL from the Montreal Canadiens to honor the first player in league history to score 50 goals in 50 games, 50 goals in a season and 500 goals in a career.

Art Ross Trophy

Top point scorer in the regular season. Arthur Howie Ross, former manager-coach of the Boston Bruins, presented the trophy to the NHL in 1947.

Conn Smythe Trophy

Most valuable player in the playoffs, as voted by the Professional Hockey Writers' Association at the conclusion of the final game in the Stanley Cup Final. The Smythe Trophy was presented by Maple Leaf Gardens Limited in1964 to honor Conn Smythe, the former coach, manager, president and owner-governor of the Toronto Maple Leafs.

Chapter 8
Off the Ice

Hockey has come a long way since players stuffed magazines into their socks to protect their shins, but thought nothing of going onto the ice bare-headed. The safety of everyone is now high-priority. Player and team collectibles go back to long before the birth of the NHL and are constantly evolving. Newspapers reported on games from the earliest days, radio began in 1923 and television's *Hockey Night in Canada* is 65 years old. Today, however, the internet allows every minute of every game to be followed by fans worldwide.

Seventy years ago, few players wore helmets and padding was minimal.

Evolution of Equipment

1

From helmets to skates, no 21st-century hockey player would consider taking to the ice without several layers of clothing, helmet, sticks, gloves, and padding. Hockey equipment has evolved as technology changed and continues to do so with safety being the prime concern.

In the earliest days of hockey, little thought was given to equipment. It's not surprising to learn that as the game developed, the first area players tried to protect was their shins.

In the 1880s, players started using strips of leather or felt, reinforced with thin lengths of cane, to protect their shins from errant sticks and pucks. It would take another decade before players began to design protection for their knees. The original kneepads consisted of large squares of leather or canvas, reinforced with felt. By the 1920s, knee and shin pads were attached together. The material flexibility of the knee and shin pads improved greatly with the development of plastics and Velcro after World War II.

Hockey pictures from the 19th century show players wearing gloves that look similar to what a modern oil-rigger might wear, with the long gauntlet running up the arm. Protection from the cold was their main purpose. Around the 1900 season, players began to wear padded leather gloves, the padding made up of animal hair and felt. Some gloves included rattan reeds over the wrist portion to add extra protection. Bill O'Brien, trainer for both the Montreal Maroons and the Montreal Canadiens, claims to have invented the reinforced thumb that is now standard on hockey gloves. According to O'Brien, the development came about after Babe Siebert broke his thumb in 1931. Unable to play without some form of added protection, O'Brien added a shoehorn to the thumb of Siebert's glove.

Harness makers for horses originally provided clues as to how hockey players could protect their shoulders and back against injury. One of the all-time greats of the game, Fred "Cyclone" Taylor, was said to be in a harness shop in Renfrew, Ontario, in 1910 when he noticed how felt was

1: Boston's Eddie Shore donned one of hockey's first helmets after a hit he delivered fractured the skull of Toronto's Ace Bailey.

2: No one but the goalie (in cricket pads) shows any signs of visible protection in the 1901 photograph of the Winnipeg Victorias.

3: New York Rangers teammates Bryan Hextall, Neil Colville and Lynn Patrick wore their elbow pads outside their sweaters in the 1940s.

4: Eddie Shore delivered the career-ending hit on Toronto Star Ace Bailey in December 1933 and, thereafter, always wore a helmet.

2

3

4

5: Cyclone Taylor is considered professional hockey's first superstar and was one of the first players to add protective padding to his equipment.

6: Tyler Seguin of the Dallas Stars wears state-of-the-art equipment: the now mandatory visor on his helmet, short gloves, wrist protectors and composite stick.

7: More NHL players began wearing helmets after the death of Bill Masterton (19) seen here being covered by Tim Horton of the Toronto Maple Leafs.

8: These skates worn by Frank Mahovlich include the protective plastic cap on the back of the blade that became mandatory in the NHL in 1964–65.

9: A Spalding hockey stick from the early 1900s.

used to protect horses from the weight of the saddle. Taylor took some scraps of felt from the shop and sewed them into his undershirt around the shoulders and down his back. Another legend claims that Taylor's mother had begun sewing felt and corset supports into his sweater and undergarments when he played junior hockey in Listowel, Ontario. Felt and leather continued to be the main material used to make shoulder pads until after World War II, which saw the creation of such materials as plastic and fiberglass.

Hockey players first used elbow pads around 1910. The original pads were simple in design, consisting of an elastic bandage for support with strips of felt to protect against bruising. They were worn on the outside of the uniform until the 1940s, when too many injuries were resulting from elbows to the face. Even after elbow pads were required to be worn inside the sweater, there was an effort to ensure that pads met certain criteria and were not simply brass knuckles worn on the elbows. This led the to the NHL passing a rule prior to the 1958–59 hockey season that became known as the "dangerous equipment rule." The idea behind it was to force manufacturers to design pads with the idea of absorbing impact and not inflicting pain. Toward this end, the new ruling made illegal any equipment containing metal.

Despite the development of safety equipment over the years, one of the most vulnerable areas of the player was left bare for a long time. There were spurts in which players would don a helmet, such as after the Eddie Shore and Ace Bailey incident that saw Bailey's career (and almost his life) ended due to a fractured skull. Shore himself donned a helmet after that, but few players followed his lead until another tragedy more than 34 years later.

On January 13, 1968, a mere two weeks after suffering a serious concussion, Bill Masterton of the Minnesota North Stars suffered another blow to his head. He spent 30 hours in the hospital before dying from his injuries. Following Masterton's death, a number of players began to wear helmets. Plastic and foam had replaced leather in the construction of hockey helmets, but there were no safety standards until after Masterton's death. During the 1970s, helmets became mandatory for players in the college and junior ranks, and the NHL made helmets mandatory for any player who signed a contract after June 1, 1979. In 1992 players had to sign a waiver to be exempt from wearing a helmet and Craig MacTavish became the NHL's last bareheaded player.

Hockey helmets were essentially designed to eliminate skull fractures, and have been very successful in that regard. With the rising incidence of concussions, and increased awareness of their long-term effects, new helmets, with improved liners to lessen the force of impacts, have been introduced. As around 70 percent of players already wear helmets with visors, the NHL made them mandatory beginning in 2013–14 for all players with fewer than 25 games of experience in the league. Like the helmet rule, veteran players currently playing without visors can still do so.

Hockey Sticks

The hockey stick, with its long wooden shaft and thin, narrow blade, is thought to have been modeled on the hurley—the weapon used in the traditional Irish game of hurling. Hockey sticks in the early 1900s would have been a heavy, well-oiled, one-piece stick carved from yellow birch, hornbeam, rock elm or white ash. Two-piece and three-piece wooden sticks (with a fitted blade and shaft) were introduced over the next 50 years.

Aluminum sticks were introduced in 1979. These were replaced by composite or fiberglass/graphite sticks in the 1980s. Today, composite sticks have superior weight and feel.

As far back as the 1940s, future NHL star Andy Bathgate experimented with curved blades, but found little acceptance. When Chicago Blackhawks teammates Stan Mikita and Bobby Hull started bending blades in the early 1960s, however, a new era in scoring was begun.

Hockey on the Air

Though he wasn't actually the first man to broadcast a hockey game, Foster Hewitt's skill at doing so saw both his and the game's popularity reach new heights. Radio was the rage in the 1930s and '40s, but television began to take over in the 1950s and _Hockey Night In Canada_ has been a TV staple since 1952.

1

I n his 1967 autobiography _Foster Hewitt: In His Own Words_, Hewitt wrote about the first time he called a hockey game on the radio. He recalled the date as March 22, 1923. That date has since been repeated many times, and in many sources. The game is usually described as an Eastern Canada Allan Cup playoff game between the Kitchener Greenshirts and the Parkdale Canoe Club at Toronto's Mutual Street Arena. Hewitt even recorded a recreation of the introduction to that broadcast for a _Hockey Night in Canada_ commemorative album in the early 1970s.

In interviews in his later years, Hewitt sometimes admitted that he may have gotten a few of the details wrong in his recollection of his first broadcast. As it turns out, Hewitt's first radio broadcast was actually of a game between the Kitchener Greenshirts and the Toronto Argonauts hockey team … and it aired on February 16, 1923—five weeks before the date he had remembered! Even so, the game Hewitt called that night was not the first hockey game to be broadcast live. CFCA, a radio station owned by the _Toronto Star_ newspaper where Hewitt was employed, had put the first hockey game on the air on February 8, 1923. Its broadcaster was another _Toronto Star_ employee, Norman Albert. That night, Albert was at the Mutual Street Arena to call the third period of an OHA intermediate playoff game between Midland and North Toronto.

On February 14, 1923, CFCA was rinkside again, covering the third period of a game between the Ottawa Senators and the Toronto St. Pats. This was the first broadcast of an NHL hockey game and it likely featured Albert calling the play-by-play again. Hewitt made his first broadcast two nights later, and the rest was history. CFCA continued to broadcast the third period of virtually every senior OHA game (and three more NHL games) at the Mutual Street Arena through to the end of the hockey season in March. Albert, however, called only one more game as Hewitt became the voice of hockey in Toronto.

With the opening of Maple Leaf Gardens on November 12, 1931, Hewitt's popularity began to expand. His _General Motors Hockey Broadcasts_ were being heard on a handful of stations across Ontario. (In Quebec, Montreal Maroons and Montreal Canadiens games were also on the air.) By 1933, Hewitt was on his way to becoming the voice of hockey

3

Radio Pioneers

The first broadcast of a complete hockey game occurred in Winnipeg on February 22, 1923. It aired on CJCG, which was owned and operated by the _Manitoba Free Press_. The Winnipeg Falcons beat the Port Arthur Bearcats 4-1 in a senior amateur playoff game. The broadcaster that night is unknown.

With much of the early history of hockey broadcasting recorded incorrectly due to Foster Hewitt's error in dates, Pete Parker's broadcast on CKCK (owned by the _Regina Leader_) on March 14, 1923 is sometimes credited as the first. It wasn't, but it was the first time all 60 minutes of a professional hockey game were on the air. The Edmonton Eskimos beat the Regina Capitals 1-0 in a Western Canada Hockey League playoff game.

The first Stanley Cup broadcasts actually predate these pioneering events, though they weren't truly live. In March of 1922, Vancouver Sun radio station CJCE read telegraphed reports from Toronto over the airwaves to fans in British Columbia.

RADIO FANS ENABLED TO FOLLOW HOCKEY GAME BY LEADER'S AID

2

Beside the 7,000 wild-eyed hockey fans who saw the Edmonton Eskimos defeat the Capitals at the Stadium last night, hundreds of others in all parts of the country within a 2,000-mile radius heard about the game. The _Leader_ radio station, CKCK, was responsible.

The broadcasting of the game was an innovation in radio circles in Western Canada and it proved a great success.

An announcer watched the game from within a padded cabinet in the bandstand at the Stadium. A transparent front enabled him to watch every movement made by the players and he told the fans of every play. By speaking into a telephone receiver connected with The _Leader_ radio room, he was able to tell the fans the sounds and made them much louder.

"This is CKCK speaking, operated by the Regina Morning _Leader_ at Regina, Sask., broadcasting the hockey game between the Edmonton Eskimos and the Regina Capitals in the first game of the playoff for the Western Canada hockey league championship. There is no score at the end of the first period."

This was the announcement made by the announcer at the end of the first period, and when he finally announced that the game was over and the Eskimos had won by a single goal, cheers were emitted by the El-

monton backers and sighs by the Capitals' friends.

Although the sending booth was heavily padded it was impossible to keep out the cheering from the vast throng in the rink and such expressions as "Come on Traub," "Lucky others" "Shoot, Keats," and many offside in the when Simpson scored from a noise was so loud that the announcer could not tell that Referee Skinner Poulin had over-ruled the second period decision in awarding a goal referee's an easy matter to tell which way the majority of the fans were pulling. Time after time the spectators could be heard cheering the Caps on but the Edmonton fans at the game let themselves be heard in no uncertain voice when Gagne scored the decid-ing count.

Heard at Moose Jaw

MOOSE JAW, March 14.—Moose Jaw fans displayed a keen interest in the Eskimo-Capitals battle in Regina tonight, both in the flesh and in the spirit. The fleshlings made the journey to the Capital on a special C.P.R. train with tickets for the Stadium in their pockets. The spirit-ually inclined fans, who were either unable to procure tickets, heard the game, including cheers, squeals and other emanations, over The _Leader's_ broadcasting route. It's a toss-up which were winners.

4

in Canada when the first national radio network started up on January 1. Twenty stations across the country were now carrying Saturday night games from both Toronto and Montreal. By season's end, the network had grown to 33 stations with an audience estimated at 1 million people. Surveys showed that 72 percent of all radios in Canada were tuned to hockey broadcasts on a Saturday night.

Throughout the 1930s and '40s, radio continued to captivate hockey fans across Canada. Hewitt called Maple Leafs games, while Charlie Harwood, Doug Smith and Michel Normandin called the games from Montreal. At the same time, American teams were starting to air their games, described by such broadcasting pioneers as Bob Elson and Lloyd Pettit in Chicago, Bert Lee in New York, Fred Cusick in Boston and Budd Lynch in Detroit.

Television arrived on the hockey scene to stay with the birth of *Hockey Night in Canada* in 1952. In preparation, an experimental video

5

6

Early TV Broadcasts

Although hockey on television was new to most Canadians when *Hockey Night in Canada* went on the air, transmission of hockey games had occurred as far back as October 29, 1938. That night, the second and third periods of a game from Harringay arena in London, England were aired.

On February 25, 1940, an experimental TV station in New York, W2XBS, broadcast a hockey game between the New York Rangers and the Montreal Canadiens to 300 fans. In November of 1946, KTLA in Los Angeles aired games from the Pacific Coast League and in the 1946–47 NHL season, the Rangers were the first NHL team to have their home games on television. Bud Palmer began calling Rangers games on WPIX in the early 1950s. From 1957 to 1960, he provided the play-by-play when CBS aired a Saturday afternoon "Game of the Week" from the American NHL cities of New York, Chicago, Detroit or Boston.

transmission of a Memorial Cup hockey game took place from Maple Leaf Gardens in April of 1952. This telecast was a closed circuit viewing for the benefit of executives from CBC television, Imperial Oil and the MacLaren advertising agency. All were impressed by Hewitt's call of the game. Broadcasts began for real on October 11, 1952. Rene Lecavalier, a French-language broadcasting legend in Montreal, called the first game when the Canadiens hosted the Detroit Red Wings. Later that season, Danny Gallivan would begin broadcasting English-language telecasts from the Montreal Forum.

The Toronto Maple Leafs made their TV debut when they hosted the Boston Bruins on November 1. Foster Hewitt called the game, with his son Bill taking over on radio. In October 1958, Bill Hewitt took over the TV broadcasts. Foster stayed on as the first Toronto "color" man until returning to radio in 1961. CBC began broadcasting games in color in 1966–67 and, after years starting broadcasts with games already in progress, the CBC finally began to air games in their entirety in 1968–69.

In recent years, team and league web sites have become increasingly important ways to cover NHL clubs. The NHL also has its own TV network and offers the NHL Center Ice digital television subscription package featuring regular season games that are played outside of local viewing area. But the biggest news in hockey broadcasting came in November of 2013 when the NHL signed a 12-year, $5.2 billion deal with Rogers Communications giving the company exclusive broadcast and multimedia rights to Canadian games, including control of the iconic *Hockey Night in Canada* broadcast on Saturday nights.

1: Danny Gallivan broadcast hockey games 1952–84.

2: Owned by the *Regina Leader*, radio station CKCK aired the first full hockey game commentary in 1923.

3: Foster Hewitt at the mic early in his career.

4: Modern hockey broadcasters and commentators follow storylines onto the ice and into the studio: (top) CBC announcers Kelly Hrudey (left) and Ron MacLean (right) chat with Brian Burke in 2004.

5: A former Sabres player, then a team broadcaster, Jim Lorentz interviews Henrik Tallinder.

6: Comcast SportsNet anchors Neil Hartman (left) and James Brown.

From the first hockey cards—available in cigarette packages in 1910—to bobblehead dolls and game-worn artifacts, there is no shortage of memorabilia for fans to collect. What was once little more than a young fan's hobby the collectibles market is now a multi-million dollar industry.

1

Sports collectibles have come a long way since the days when kids put cards in their bicycle spokes, flipped them for distance or accuracy, and scrambled them in schoolyards. By the late 1980s, sports collectibles had become big business.

Still popular today, bobblehead dolls first appeared in the 1950s. By 1960, Major League Baseball had created bobblehead dolls in every team uniform … though, to many fans, the oversized head always looked the same. Throughout the 1960s, ceramic bobblehead dolls were produced in others sports and for cartoon characters, but the craze died out by the 1970s. It was reborn in the 1990s with cheaper—but better—materials that allowed bobbleheads to provide much more accurate likenesses. Again, baseball led the way, but today there is no shortage of NHL bobblehead dolls for every team and superstar player.

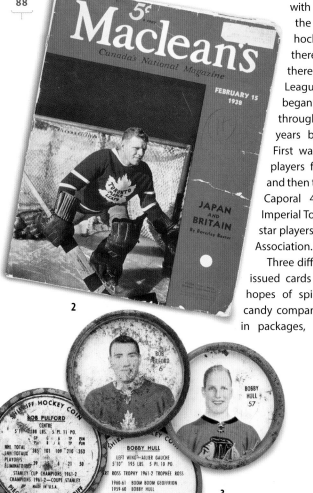

For hockey, the collectible market all began with hockey cards. To appreciate the rich, colorful tradition of hockey cards, consider that there were hockey cards before there was a National Hockey League. Cigarette companies began issuing hockey cards throughout Canada in 1910, seven years before the NHL debuted. First was a 32-card set featuring players from the 1909–10 season and then there was a 1910–11 Sweet Caporal 45-card set (included in Imperial Tobacco cigarettes) featured star players from the National Hockey Association.

Three different cigarette companies issued cards from 1910 to 1913 with hopes of spiking sales. In the 1920s candy companies began to insert cards in packages, and in the 1930s gum companies, in particular O-Pee-Chee and World Wide Gum, began to use hockey cards to boost their products in the marketplace.

The modern era of collecting starts with the introduction of the 1951–52 Parkhurst set. Topps hockey cards debuted as a test in 1954–55. Topps (an American company) didn't seem convinced it was an effective method of selling chewing gum. The company didn't issue card sets in 1955–56 or 1956–57, but then came back in 1957–58. As a general rule in the 1950s, Topps issued cards of players from American teams and Parkhurst issued cards of players from the Montreal Canadiens and Toronto Maple Leafs.

After the 1963–64 season, Parkhurst left the hockey card business. Starting in 1964–65, Topps began issuing cards of players from every team. Topps' designs in the 1960s were unique. For the 1964–65 season they issued an oversized set that featured 110-cards of $2\frac{1}{2}$" x $4\frac{11}{16}$". Dubbed

Tabletop Hockey

Donald H. Munro built he earliest type of tabletop hockey game in his Toronto home in 1932. Made of wood and scrap metal found in his neighborhood, Munro built his first game as a Christmas present for his children at a time when he could not afford to buy gifts. Munro soon built a handful of these wooden games on consignment for Eaton's department store in Toronto and they became an instant success.

The innovation that led to metal rods and slots was introduced in Sweden during the 1930s, but the first modern-style table top game in Canada was introduced by the Eagle Toy Company of Montreal in 1954. Eagle's National Hockey Game featured players printed in color on flat metal cutouts who stood on a surface that resembled ice. Both Munro and Eagle remained the design leaders and created tabletop hockey games well into the 1970s.

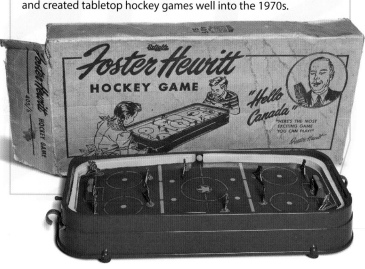

1: An NHL lunchbox from the 1970s.

2: Toronto Maple Leafs goalie Turk Broda graces the cover of *Maclean's* magazine.

3: Young fans prized Shirriff Hockey Coins in the 1960s.

2

3

McFarlane Toys

Todd McFarlane of Calgary, Alberta hoped to be a professional baseball player. When that career didn't pan out, he focused on his art. In the late 1980s, he worked on Spider-Man for Marvel Comics, then launched his own franchise with Spawn. He formed his own toy company in 1994 to better market his characters. In 1998, McFarlane became a minority owner of the Edmonton Oilers.

Sports is a major part of McFarlane Toys, with the company producing officially licensed action figures for Major League Baseball, the NFL, the NBA and the NHL. McFarlane's sports series began with hockey when two product lines were introduced in 2000. Since then, dozens of players from emerging stars to established veterans to hockey legends have been reproduced in amazing detail. Every player is sculpted in an action pose and the faces are astonishingly lifelike. Each figure wears an accurate team uniform and is dressed in the exact type of equipment they actually use.

O-Pee-Chee and Topps sets became virtually identical. During the late 1980s and 1990s, when companies like Upper Deck got into the business, hockey cards got glitzier, but older cards remain collectable for their rarity and nostalgia.

Similar to old hockey cards, Beehive photos (first issued in 1933) evoke a special kind of nostalgia. Kids of that era would tear the labels off the Beehive corn syrup bottles and send them in for the photo cards. Hockey legend Gordie Howe collected these cards as a child in Saskatchewan and still laments that a relative threw away his collection. Bobby Hull was a Beehive collector and is fond of telling stories of rummaging through neighbors' garbage looking for the corn syrup labels. Beehive suspended issuing photos in 1944, and again in 1963, before stopping for good in 1967. Shirriff hockey "coins" of the 1960s have similar nostalgic value for those old enough to remember the era of the "Original Six."

Today, the hottest colletctibles are game-worn artifacts and autographs. These days, autograph sessions are highly organized affairs and obtaining a signature can be expensive. Another recent trend has seen players or their families selling lifetime collections at auction. Items once belonging to hockey legends ranging from Jack Stewart, Buddy O'Connor and Maurice Richard from the 1930s, '40s and '50s to Guy Lafleur, Clark Gilles and Luc Robitaille from the 1970s, '80s and '90s have all gone under the gavel. Bobby Hull's Stanley Cup ring from 1961 sold for $85,000 US, while a game-used 1971 Jean Beliveau stick fetched $17,500. But nothing can match the sale of Paul Henderson's sweater from the 1972 Canada–USSR Summit Series. It went for $1.25 million!

"Tall Boys" by collectors, these larger sized cards often suffered from bent corners, making a mint-condition set rare and therefore highly collectible. (No other card of that size was issued until 1993–94 when Fleer introduced a set called Power Play.) Another valuable Topps set from this era is the 1966–67 set. It featured only 66 cards, but includes Bobby Orr's rookie card.

Orr's Boston teammate Phil Esposito has an unusual card from the 1971–72 set in that the pair of plaid pants he is wearing beneath his hockey sweater is clearly visible!

O-Pee-Chee (a Canadian company) started to make hockey cards again in 1968-69. O-Pee-Chee used the Topps design, but always had more cards in the set, a reflection of hockey's popularity in Canada. That makes those O-Pee-Chee sets very popular with collectors of rookie cards. For example, the 1970–71 O-Pee-Chee sets had rookie cards for Bobby Clarke and Darryl Sittler while the 1971–72 set featured Marcel Dionne and Guy Lafleur and Topps sets did not. Beginning in 1974–75,

4: Metal table hockey men from the Original Six era. The switch to plastic players came in the early 1970s.

5: Canada Post has issued several series of stamps depicting NHL All-Stars.

6: Big-game tickets are also much in demand for collectors.

7: Canadiens, Maple Leafs and Red Wings pendants.

Stories Behind the Treasures

Programs, telegrams, advertisements, schedules, collector cards, and drawings: they all provide one more way to make the history of the National Hockey League come alive. Contained throughout this book are exact facsimiles of important objects that document every era of the game.

DAN BAIN TELEGRAM 1901; EASTERN CANADA HOCKEY ASSOCIATION SCHEDULE 1907–08

(see pages 16–17) In the early days of Stanley Cup competition, telegrams and telegraph wires were the fastest way to keep up to date on the goings on in other cities. Dan Bain, an early era legend who was inducted into the Hockey Hall of Fame in 1949, received this telegram after leading the Winnipeg Victorias to a Stanley Cup victory over the Montreal Shamrocks in 1901. Bain and the Victorias were Stanley Cup champions in 1896, 1901 and 1902. The Eastern Canada Amateur Hockey Association was the top league in hockey from 1905–06 through 1907–08. Despite its name, the league became open to professional players in 1906–07. It was one of a series of amateur and professional leagues that were the forerunners of the NHL.

JOE HALL CONTRACT, 1918–19; COLLECTION OF PRE-NHL HOCKEY CARDS

(see pages 16–17) Joe Hall's contract with the Montreal Canadiens for the 1918–19 season is standard for the early era. Hall received a $600 salary, plus an additional $100 that gave the Canadiens the first right to re-sign him the following season.

Hockey cards for Newsy Lalonde, Jack Laviolette and Fred "Cyclone" Taylor actually date from the first season of the National Hockey Association. All were still active when the league was re-formed as the NHL, though Cyclone Taylor was starring in the rival Pacific Coast Hockey Association.

SOUVENIR PROGRAM FROM 1924–25 STANLEY CUP SERIES

(see page 16–17) During the early years of the NHL, the final series for the Stanley Cup pitted the eastern-based NHL's championship team against the champions of the major professional leagues out west. Because travel from coast to coast by train could take an entire week, each series was played in one city alternating yearly between the east and west. The Stanley Cup series of 1925 saw the defending champion Montreal Canadiens of the NHL travel to British Columbia to face the Victoria Cougars of the Western Canada Hockey League. Victoria coach Lester Patrick rotated two sets of forward lines fairly evenly throughout the series, while the Canadiens relied almost exclusively on their star combination of Howie Morenz, Aurel Joliat and Billy Boucher. The result was a three-games-to-one victory for Victoria in the best-of-five series.

NHL SCHEDULE, 1933–34; TURRET CIGARETTES HOCKEY CONSTEST LEAFLET; LES CANADIENS EN CARICATURE, 1930

(see pages 32–33) The Great Depression took its toll on the NHL. The league had already lost one franchise by 1933–34, and the original Ottawa Senators would be gone for good by the end of that year. Times were tough all over, and though crowds were down at NHL rinks, hockey still offered some hope. *Les Canadiens en Caricature*, which seems aimed at a more upscale audience, made hockey players look as glamorous as movie stars. Turret Cigarettes offered cash prizes (which doubled if the estimates were sent on empty cigarette packs!) that represented several years' salary at the time for fans that correctly guessed how many goals each team would score during the 1931–32 season.

TORONTO MAPLE LEAFS STANLEY CUP INSCRIPTION NOTE

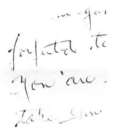

(see pages 32–33) The fact that the names of individual players are engraved on the Stanley Cup is a big reason why hockey's ultimate prize has such mythical appeal. Team names have been engraved since 1893, but the Montreal Wanderers were the first to engrave player names in 1907. It has been an annual tradition since 1924. With larger rosters these days, there are rules about what it takes to be included on the Cup, and teams are restricted to listing no more than a total of 53 players and front office personnel. There were no such restrictions necessary in the 1940s, when the Toronto Maple Leafs won the Cup five times and even engraved the names of children of prominent executives who served as team mascots.

RICHARD RIOT FORFEIT NOTE; 1958–59 NHL FINAL STATISTICS BOOKLET

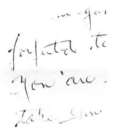

(see pages 32–33) The Detroit Red Wings and the Montreal Canadiens dominated the NHL in the 1950s. Detroit won the Stanley Cup four times from 1950 to 1955, followed by Montreal's five wins in a row from 1956 to 1960. One of the darkest moments in NHL history occurred during a game between these two rivals on March 17, 1955, when Canadiens fans rioted to protest NHL President Clarence Campbell's decision to suspend Maurice Richard. The Canadiens were forced to default the game that night, and went on to lose the Stanley Cup to Detroit a month later. The fallout from the Richard Riot may well have sparked the Canadiens to the greatness that saw them dominate the rest of the decade. The final statistics from the 1958–59 season clearly show just how dominating these Montreal teams were.

CALIFORNIA SEALS JOIN THE NHL BOOKLET

(see pages 32–33) Despite its image of sun and surf, a long tradition of minor league hockey made California a natural target for NHL expansion in 1867–68. The Los Angeles entry went to transplanted Canadian Jack Kent Cooke, while the California Seals were owned by jet-setting beachboy Barry Van Gerbig. Van Gerbig and his partners purchased the rights to the San Francisco Seals team of the Western Hockey League and moved their base of operations across the Bay to Oakland. The decision to leave San Francisco proved to be a mistake, as the team never really established an identity in Oakland. Owners, GMs, coaches and players all came and went quickly during an 11-year existence that saw just two playoff appearances and included revolving name changes between California Seals, Oakland Seals and California Golden Seals.

STANLEY CUP SPECIFICATION DRAWING, c1958

(see pages 50–51) The custom of engraving the winners' names on the Stanley Cup forced it to grow with the addition of more and more silver bands. Between 1928 and 1947, the Cup grew into a long, narrow cylinder sometimes referred to as "the elephant's leg." The silver bands from this tall, skinny trophy were remounted in 1948 onto a new bottom section that gave the Cup its now-familiar barrel look. However, with no standards in place, the new bands that continued to be added quickly filled the Cup's expanded space. It was obvious that something more had to be done. The specs on this drawing show an early attempt to standardize the bands on the lower section of the Stanley Cup. The current design, which was unveiled in 1958, is quite similar to this drawing, though the new barrel was both taller and wider.

TOPIX COMICS, PATRICKS' EDITION MARCH 1947

(see pages 50–51) Though their father Lester was a legend both as a player and in the front office, Lynn and Muzz Patrick grew up in a decidedly non-hockey environment. Lynn was a star football and basketball player, but did not play competitive hockey until joining a senior team in Montreal in 1933–34. His father feared being accused of nepotism and was reluctant to let Lynn join the New York Rangers, but did so the following year after other general managers began expressing interest in him. Muzz Patrick was also a versatile athlete who starred in track, basketball, football, cycling, and boxing. He joined his brother on the Rangers three years later, in 1937. Lynn's story is told quite faithfully in this 1947 *TOPIX Comic*.

JACQUES PLANTE GOALKEEPING BOOK

(see pages 20–21) Statistically, there is no question that Jacques Plante rates among the greatest goaltenders in the game. When he left the NHL in 1973, his 437 victories ranked second all time, and his 82 shutouts ranked fourth. Very few others have passed him since, and no one has ever bettered his record of seven Vezina Trophy wins. Plante was also a Stanley Cup champion six times, and, of course, he championed the use of the goalie mask against the wishes of coaches and league executives who were dead set against it. Late in his career, Plante groomed fellow netminder Bernie Parent for stardom. Though he was considered a first-class eccentric, Plante had a knack for teaching as his thoughtful book on goaltending instruction certainly attests.

ᴗeven years
ᴌes was announced ⅼ
ɔr years saying thɛ
ꜱ evident to me thɛ
ansion will improve
ᴨvestment from
ᴉneꜱꜱ

WHA EXPANSION BULLETIN; RONALD REAGAN LETTER, 1982

(see pages 50–51) John A. Ziegler, Jr. graduated from the University of Michigan in 1957, and began doing legal work for Bruce Norris, the Detroit Red Wings, and the Detroit Olympia in 1959. He joined the NHL Board of Governors as an alternate governor for the Red Wings in 1966, and in September 1977 succeeded Clarence Campbell to become the fourth NHL president in League history. During his tenure as NHL president, Ziegler forged a strong working relationship with the NHL Players' Association and helped to negotiate the entry of four World Hockey Association teams into the NHL in 1979. He remained as president until the end of the 1991–92 season.

NHL OFFICIAL SCHEDULE, 1991–92; BLACKHAWKS VS. LEAFS PLAYING ROSTERS, 1994

(see pages 50–51) The NHL celebrated its 75th season in 1991–92 by welcoming its first new franchise in more than a decade. The San Jose Sharks marked the beginning of a wave of new "sun belt" teams as the NHL looked to expand its marketplace. The decade also featured impressive performances from some of the NHL's "Original Six" franchises. The Toronto Maple Leafs reached Conference finals in both 1993 and 1994, while the Montreal Canadiens celebrated the Stanley Cup's centennial in 1993 with the 24th championship in franchise history. The New York Rangers ended a 54-year Stanley Cup drought with a win in 1994, and the Detroit Red Wings ended a 42-year jinx in 1997, then repeated with another Cup win in 1998.

GENERAL MOTORS HOCKEY BROADCAST GUIDE

(see pages 76–77) Toronto Maple Leafs owner Conn Smythe was quick to realize the potential of radio. He backed Foster Hewitt's broadcasts in the late 1920s over the protestations of other Leafs directors who were worried that giving away games for free on the radio would hurt ticket sales. As Smythe suspected, radio broadcasts made Toronto's team more popular than ever. General Motors also realized the potential of hockey on the radio as a marketing tool. By sponsoring broadcasts from coast-to-coast, they got a celebrity in Hewitt to help sell their cars and a nation full of car dealerships to promote their broadcasts. Their *Hockey Broadcast Guide* promoted both products and made the broadcasts more "interactive." It was a multimedia synergy worth of the Internet generation!

ASSORTED MEMORABLIA

(see pages 76-77) Hockey cards, which began as inserts in cigarette cartons, were being packaged with gum and candy by the time the cards in this assortment were available in the 1920s and 30s. (The Stanley Cup card is from a 1970s series that included all the NHL trophies, and which could be turned over and combined to form a picture of Bobby Orr.) Modern hockey memorabilia includes many items that are manufactured to become collectibles, such as the elaborate tickets created by the Toronto Maple Leafs to commemorate the night of their final ever game at Maple Leaf Gardens on February 13, 1999 and their first game at the Air Canada Centre one week later.

EQUIPMENT ADVERTISEMENT (DATE UNKNOWN)

(see pages 76–77) No matter how equipment evolves, the heart of hockey is the stick and the puck. In the very earliest days of the game, sticks were hacked from roots or tree branches. The first true pucks were simply rubber balls sliced flat … though folks playing shinny might also cut their pucks from tree branches. This advertisement for "regulation" sticks and pucks from the Spalding sporting goods company probably dates from the 1890s or 1900s. Back then, a top stick could be purchased for 75¢. Today, the top composite hockey sticks sell for as much as $250. The inflation rate for pucks has been a lot less severe.

1: A selection of collectable cards depicting hockey stars from the first decade of the last century.

FRANK PATRICK of Renfrew Club   PERCY LESUEUR of Ottawa Club   G. ROBERTS of Ottawa Club   BARNEY HOLDEN of Shamrock Club   P GLASS of Wanderers Club   EDGAR DEY of Haileybury Club   MARTIN WALSH of Ottawa Club   ART ROSS of Haileybury Club

BRUCE STUART of Ottawa Club   NICK BAWLF of Haileybury Club   J. JONES of Cobalt Club   ERNEST RUSSELL of Wanderers Club   JACK LAVIOLETTE of Canadian Club   RILEY HERN of Wanderers Club   D. PITRE of Canadian Club   SKINNER POULIN of Canadian Club

JACK MARSHALL of Wanderers Club   BRUCE RIDPATH of Ottawa Club   J. MARSHALL of Shamrock Club   NEWSY LALONDE of Renfrew Club   FRANK PATRICK of Renfrew Club   PERCY LESUEUR of Ottawa Club   G. ROBERTS of Ottawa Club   BARNEY HOLDEN of Shamrock Club

ED. DECARY of Canadian Club   TOM DUNDERDALE of Shamrock Club   FRED. TAYLOR of Renfrew Club   JOS CATTARINICH of Canadian Club   BRUCE STUART of Ottawa Club   NICK BAWLF of Haileybury Club   J. JONES of Cobalt Club   ERNEST RUSSELL of Wanderers Club

A CAMPBELL of Cobalt Club   H. H. RYLAND of Wanderers Club   HERB. CLARK of Cobalt Club   ART ROSS of Haileybury Club   ED. DECARY of Canadian Club   TOM DUNDERDALE of Shamrock Club   FRED. TAYLOR of Renfrew Club   JOS CATTARINICH of Canadian Club

ART. BERNIER of Canadian Club   LESTER PATRICK of Renfrew Club   FRED LAKE of Ottawa Club   P MORAN of Haileybury Club   C. TOMS of Cobalt Club   E. JOHNSTON of Wanderers Club   HORACE GAUL of Haileybury Club   HAROLD McNAMARA of Cobalt Club

Picture Credits

The publishers would like to thank the following sources for their kind permission to reproduce the pictures in this book.